London 2012
training guide
Swimming

First published by Carlton Books Limited 2011
Copyright © 2011 Carlton Books Limited

London 2012 emblem(s) © The London Organising Committee of the Olympic
Games and Paralympic Games Ltd (LOCOG) 2007. London 2012 Pictograms
© LOCOG 2009. All rights reserved.

Carlton Books Limited,
20 Mortimer Street,
London, W1T 3JW

A CIP catalogue record for this book is available from the British Library.
10 9 8 7 6 5 4 3 2 1

ISBN: 978-1-84732-733-8

Printed in China

FSC
www.fsc.org
MIX
Paper from
responsible sources
FSC® C101537

Editor: Matthew Lowing
Design Direction: Darren Jordan
Design: Fresh Flame
Editorial: Richard Gilbert and Chris Parker
Picture Research: Paul Langan
Illustrations: Glyn Walton
Production: Karin Kolbe

Roger Guttridge is one of the UK's leading swimming journalists and a former press officer
to the Great Britain Swim Team. He is currently the principal news and feature writer for
Swimming Times magazine.

Kelvin Juba has over 40 years experience of working within swimming as a writer, television
adviser and commentator. He is the author of over 10 books on the sport including *Get Fit:
Swimming* and *The Handbook of Swimming*.

London 2012 training guide

Swimming

From beginner to champion

Roger Guttridge and Kelvin Juba

CARLTON

Contents

Foreword by Rebecca Adlington OBE

From a very young age I loved to swim and it was great that I soon found I was good at it. But it is a long, long way from being very good at something to becoming an Olympic champion.

I have had to make countless sacrifices to be where I am today, but I am not alone. My family gave up so much of their time and energy taking me to and from training and competitions, my coaches never stopped believing in me and instilling the self-confidence that breeds success and my team-mates and rivals made sure that I had to improve myself in competition to stay ahead of them.

This *London 2012 Training Guide* will help you to learn the basics, become more competitive, more successful and – almost certainly – more self-assured. Training, if done properly, is always hard work and in this book you will read about the various strokes and disciplines, as well as picking up tips on vital techniques such as the starts and turns.

You won't become an international champion overnight, but with hard work and practice, you might win a gold medal.

Rebecca Adlington OBE

Introduction

During an average week, more than 3.2 million people in England visit a swimming pool at least once. That's a million more than play football. Some are serious athletes, some are leisure swimmers, some simply enjoy having fun in water. Together, their numbers make swimming the most popular participation sport in the country.

The figures, taken from Sport England's 'Active People' survey, apply only to England, but swimming is no less popular in other parts of the UK – or other parts of the western world. It's also the only sport on the National Curriculum and arguably the only one that could not only save your life but save someone else's. Swimming exercises all the body's muscle groups and is ideal as a cardiovascular workout.

As both a low-impact and a non-contact sport, with a relatively low risk of injury, swimming appeals to the widest possible age range. Most children love being active in water, but swimming is also the chosen sport of millions of adults, including many elderly people, who find that it's an enjoyable as well as effective way to help them stay fit and active. A growing number of doctors recommend swimming as a suitable form of exercise for their patients.

Because of its low-impact nature and the support that water gives to the body, swimming also has a specific appeal to people with a range of physical conditions. It is one of the few sports that pregnant women can do, and it actually helps their mobility and their breathing during labour. Injured professionals from other sports commonly use swimming as a stepping stone to fitness. Obesity is no barrier to swimming and neither are learning difficulties, blindness, deafness, missing limbs, spinal injuries, arthritis, most back problems and many other conditions.

Unlike team sports, swimming is something you can do alone (under lifeguard supervision, of course). Yet for many, its social side is also one of its attractions. Joining a swimming club invariably opens the door to new friendships and related activities.

For those who wish to take their swimming more seriously, the competitive opportunities are limitless. For children, national championships start at 11 years and some competitions a year or two earlier. 'Masters' swimming offers organised competition from local through to world level, with age groups that range from 18–24 to 95–99 years or even 100-plus. Paralympic swimming is divided

Olympic silver medallist Amaury Leveaux of France performs an immaculate racing dive.

into 14 disability categories. Outside the Paralympic structure, there are also specific competitions for the blind, the deaf, Down's syndrome swimmers and organ transplantees.

You don't need to be an Olympic swimmer to take part in most of these events. Apart from being reasonably healthy and able to swim, the main requirement is that you are registered with the sport's governing body – which usually means being a member of a swimming club. For disability swimming, you will also need a classification assessment.

At the elite level, swimming was one of the nine founding sports at the first Modern Olympic Games in 1896, and has been a mainstay of the Olympic programme ever since. Each Olympic swimming final is watched by a television audience of billions, and a live audience in excess of 17,000. Such events are an inspiration to millions, and attendances at public pools invariably peak during and after the Olympic Games.

Getting started

If there's one thing you need to exercise before you put your swimming muscles to the test, it's common sense. Before you head for the pool, give some thought to what you hope to achieve in both the short term and the longer term. Whatever your aims, it is important not to over do it.

Starting Steadily

Fitness is like Rome: it can't be built in a day. However fit you used to be, however many lengths you could swim as a youngster, it inevitably takes time to regain fitness – and swimming too hard too soon is inadvisable. Even if you are already reasonably fit from some other activity, there is only one way to be 'swimming fit' – and that's in the water. The key is to be sensible, swim regularly and build up your distance and your speed gradually.

In terms of general health, if you are reasonably fit and healthy, there's probably no need to visit your GP before taking to the pool. But if you have a pre-existing condition, it may be a good idea to seek medical or specialist advice. While swimming is generally good for asthma, anyone with that condition should make sure it is well-controlled. Sensible swimming is also good for heart conditions and high blood pressure, as it boosts aerobic capacity and can lower blood pressure for a few hours afterwards – but again the condition should be well-controlled. Diabetics can obtain good advice from the British Diabetic Association, whose website lists swimming and water aerobics among its recommended activities. Epileptics should make sure

their condition is controlled and notify their teacher, coach or lifeguard before entering the water. Detailed advice on epilepsy can be found on the website swimming.org.

At the Pool

A visit to your local pool or its website will help you to plan your sessions and get started. Most public pools offer adult-only sessions and/or lane swimming, both of which offer a better opportunity to train properly than full public sessions. Many leisure centres also run courses for swimmers of various standards, such as learners, beginners and improvers. Some pools also have fitness swimming sessions, perhaps with a coach to write a programme on the board and provide technical advice.

Taking it Further

For the more able and ambitious, a swimming club will provide the perfect environment for training and, if required, competing. Most areas now have at least one swimming club with a masters or adult section or in many cases a dedicated masters club. Standards vary from club to club but most cater for a wide range of ages and abilities (see page 22 for more details on joining a club).

Olympic silver and bronze medallist Katie Hoff of the USA performs a stretching routine before a final.

The competition pool

The swimming pool in competition format is an arena transformed. Flags, turn-ropes, lane ropes, starting blocks, officials by the dozen, swimmers by the hundred. The swimming gala can be a spine-tingling, nerve-jangling experience – and at major events that feeling is intensified.

Pool Dimensions

You can't spend long in the company of swimmers without hearing talk of 'long-course' and 'short-course'. The distinction is simple but important. Long-course refers to competitions or training in a pool that is 50 metres long; short-course refers to a 25-metre pool. Many are surprised to learn that short-course times are almost invariably quicker than long-course. This is due to the brief period of acceleration as the swimmer pushes off the wall at each turn. For this reason, at least at national and international level, two distinct sets of records are maintained – long-course and short-course.

Olympic swimming takes place in a 50-metre ten-lane pool, although the two outer lanes remain unused except during the warm-up. And while short-course championships are now held at world, European and sometimes national level, it is the equivalent long-course events that are taken most seriously by coaches and swimmers.

This distinction is usually lost on the lower levels of the sport, especially in the UK, where a dearth of long-course pools means that most swimmers train in 25-metre pools and the majority of competitions are held in them. Due to the parallel use of the imperial and metric systems of measurement, Britain's stock of older pools comes in a bewildering range

Lines on the pool floor help swimmers to swim straight.

of sizes including 20 metres, 25 yards, 25 metres, 33.3 yards, 33.3 metres and 36.66 yards (the last being the yards equivalent of 33.3 metres – almost). However, the vast majority of pools built over the last thirty years conform to the 25-metre or 50-metre format.

Fast and Slow Pools

Another recurring phrase in the swimmer's vocabulary is 'fast pool' and 'slow pool'. Some pools are well known for producing more than their share of good times (and records), some for the reverse. Sheffield's Ponds Forge, which regularly hosts national and international competitions, is universally known as an especially fast pool. There are many factors involved, most of them relating to water movement. High pool walls, variable depth, poor-quality lane ropes, the lack of a spare lane at the sides and low starting blocks all militate against fast times. When swimming from deep to shallow, the water displaced by the swimmer bounces back off the slope to hamper progress slightly.

The Officials

Every gala requires a small army of officials, who are usually uniformly dressed and are ceremonially clapped as they arrive at the poolside by swimmers and spectators. The chief official is the referee and is responsible for the correct running of the competition, including disputes and disqualifications, and for signalling swimmers to prepare for their race and to take their starting position.

Other Officials Include:

- the starter, who conducts the starting procedure;
- turn judges, posted at both ends of each lane to ensure that their swimmer complies with the rules of turning;
- stroke judges, located at the sides of the pool to ensure stroke rules are complied with and to assist the turn judges;
- chief timekeeper, responsible for overseeing the timekeepers and collecting the times they have recorded;
- timekeepers, who use stopwatches or a semi-automatic timing system to record a swimmer's time;
- finish judges, posted in line with the finish to record the finishing order;
- clerk of the course, who assembles the swimmers before each race;
- chief recorder, who checks results from computer print-outs and witnesses the signing off of results by the referee;
- recorders, responsible for recording withdrawals, results, records and scores.

The latest starting blocks include an adjustable back-plate.

Pool equipment

The line of flags that appear 5 metres from each end of a competition pool is not there for decoration. They are 'turn indicators' whose purpose is to inform backstrokers when the wall is approaching. The flag rope is suspended 1.8 metres above the water surface.

Ropes and Markers

Fifteen metres from the starting end is another rope, this time without flags. This is the false start rope, which is attached to a quick-release mechanism that allows officials to drop it across the lanes in the event of a faulty start. A swimmer hitting the rope knows it's time to stop and return to the start. There has been less call for the rope since the introduction of the one-start rule in 1998, as false-starting swimmers are allowed to continue racing and disqualified

afterwards. However, the rope is still occasionally used when there is a problem at the start – a faulty starting mechanism, for example.

Most pools are equipped with anti-wave ropes that are usually rolled out only for competitions. The plastic discs along their length are designed to minimise the wash flowing between lanes. The rules specify green ropes for lanes 1 and 8, blue for lanes 2, 3, 6 and 7 and yellow for lanes 4 and 5. To aid the swimmers' orientation, the 5 metres

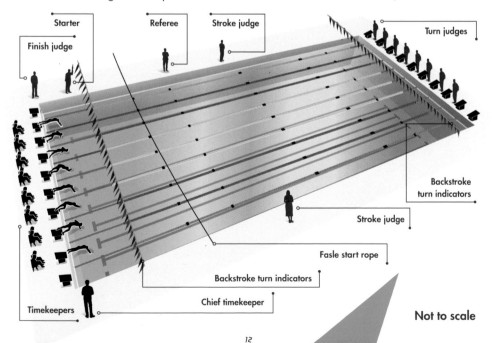

Starter

Finish judge

Referee

Stroke judge

Turn judges

Backstroke turn indicators

Stroke judge

Fasle start rope

Backstroke turn indicators

Chief timekeeper

Timekeepers

Not to scale

of rope nearest each end of the pool are coloured red. There is also a brief colour change at 15 metres – the maximum distance that a freestyler, backstroker or butterflier may remain submerged following the start or turn. Competition pools also have a 15-metre indicator of some kind on the poolside – such as a coloured brick in the wall.

Starting Blocks

Although it's not against the rules to start a race from the pool-deck or even in the water (and there are various circumstances in which it happens), the vast majority of pools provide a starting block at the end of each lane. At local level most pools still have blocks with a single platform but since the 2008 Olympic Games, world governing body, FINA, has permitted the use of blocks with an adjustable back-plate, enabling swimmers using the track-style starting technique to exert more power from their

take-off foot. Blocks also include handgrips for backstroke starts, which take place in the water. Blocks must be between 0.5 and 0.75 metres above the water.

Perfect Timing

A larger proportion of competitions are now timed electronically, providing accuracy to two decimal places – that is 0.01 seconds. The timer is activated automatically, stops when the swimmer hits the timing pad attached to the pool wall and decides not only the individual times but the placing of each swimmer. Semi-automatic timing, which can also be used as a back-up or a front-line system, involves timekeepers on each lane with a button connected to the electronic system. Manual timing with hand-held watches can still be used where electronic timing is unavailable. Ironically, manual timing tends to produce faster times because of the timekeeper's delayed reaction at the start and anticipation at the finish.

FINA rules stipulate that water temperature must be between 25°C and 28°C. It must also be constant. Inflow and outflow of water are permitted 'as long as no appreciable current or turbulence is created'.

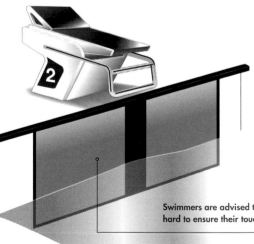

Swimmers are advised to hit the timing pad hard to ensure their touch is registered.

Swimming history

Swimming today is mostly regarded as a sport or leisure activity, but for the earliest human swimmers it was probably an aid to survival – swimming in the sea to spear fish, perhaps, or crossing a river in pursuit of prey or to escape a predator or enemy.

Origins

While swimming's true origins are lost in the mists of prehistory, references to it lie scattered throughout ancient history. Egyptian hieroglyphics from 2500 BC include pictures of people swimming a stroke that vaguely resembles the modern frontcrawl. At Nimrud in Iraq, a bas-relief from about 860 BC shows Assyrian soldiers swimming naked across a moat to escape captivity. One of several Biblical references describes the Jewish commander Jonathan and his soldiers swimming the River Jordan. A sculpture found in Perugia, Italy, features a naked figure in diving pose from 460 BC.

The Ancient Greeks had a high regard for swimming and Plato regarded a non-swimming man as uneducated. In fact, calling someone 'a man who knows not how to run or swim' in Greece was considered an insult. Greek mythology tells how Leander swam the Hellespont every night to visit his priestess lover Hero. In 1810, the poet Lord Byron famously re-created the legend by completing the 4.5-kilometre crossing from Europe to Asia at the second attempt. This in turn was replicated on 3 May 2010, 200 years later to the day, by his descendant the Hon. Charles Byron and 150 others. Turkish people hold their own Hellespont swim every

August to commemorate the final victory that established their independence from the Greeks in 1922.

A Roman Pastime

Biographies of Julius Caesar speak of his ability as a swimmer and of his escape from the battle of Alexandria in 48–47 BC by swimming to a ship, while holding a wad of important documents clear of the waves. The Romans used cork floats to help teach young men to swim and their conquering armies made good use of the skill, most notably in AD 78, when soldiers swam the Menai Strait before

launching on attack on Anglesey.

References in Anglo-Saxon and Viking literature suggest that swimming was popular in both cultures; the Vikings in particular appear to have enjoyed swimming in the sea and inland waters. The Normans, however, had little focus on swimming.

Swimming in the Middle Ages

In 1571, when swimming was popular at Oxford and Cambridge Universities, it was banned by the Vice-Chancellor at Cambridge because it led to so many drownings. Several books on swimming appeared in the sixteenth and seventeenth centuries, most notably Everard Digby's *De Arte Natandi*, first published in 1587. Digby considered swimming to be an art, comparable with medicine, war, agriculture or navigation. His recommended techniques included 'swimming like a dog', a form of sidestroke, swimming on the back using breaststroke kick and swimming underwater like a dolphin.

In the Modern Era

Benjamin Franklin was an accomplished swimmer, as onlookers discovered during his visit to London in 1726. The American independence pioneer was enjoying a cruise on the River Thames when he threw off his clothes and swam from Chelsea to Blackfriars, performing tricks on and below the water, to the delight of onlookers.

Stone tablets showing Assyrian soldiers swimming to safety in the ninth century BC – one of the first recorded depictions of swimming.

The first competitors

The first known competitive swimmers were the Japanese, who were holding races as early as 36 BC and in 1603 all schoolchildren were ordered to learn to swim and compete against other schools. Elsewhere, it was the nineteenth century before competitive swimming began to take off.

Early Competitions

In 1844 an unusual race took place in London between the breaststroking Englishman Harold Kenworthy and two native Americans, Flying Gull and Tobacco, who used a stroke similar to modern frontcrawl. 'Their style of swimming is totally un-European,' reported *The Times*. 'They lash the water violently with their arms like the sails of a windmill and beat downward with their feet, blowing with force and performing grotesque antics.' Although Flying Gull completed the 43.3-yard (39.6-metre)

The first Channel swimmer Captain Matthew Webb receives a hot drink during his historic 1875 crossing.

course in 30 seconds, Kenworthy's breaststroke saw him to victory.

The race took place at Holborn Baths, one of a handful of swimming pools that had begun to appear in British cities. It was hosted by the National Swimming Society, formed in 1837 to organise races. The first national championships took place in the same era. Tom Morris won the first one-mile title, held in the Thames between Putney and Hammersmith in 1869, in 27min 18sec.

Internationally, Australia was already emerging as a leading swimming nation, hosting the world's first modern championship in Sydney in 1846, when W. Redman won the 440 yards in 8min 43sec. A good club swimmer today could swim it in half the time. Scotland became the first country to hold a women's championship in 1892, when E. Dobbie of Glasgow won the 200 yards in 4min 25sec.

Stroke Developments

This was also a time of rapid stroke evolution. In Britain, breaststroke continued to dominate and it was this that Captain Matthew Webb used to defy the sceptics by becoming the first Channel swimmer in 1875. Webb – whose diet during the swim included coffee, beer and steak – completed the 21 miles in 21hr 45min.

Sidestroke, swum single-arm with a scissor kick, became popular as a racing stroke after 1855, when C. W. Wallis demonstrated the technique that was used by Australian aborigines. Professor Fred Beckwith adapted it to include an over-the-water arm recovery action, which won him the English championship in 1859.

Another import was the trudgeon (often spelt trudgen), introduced from South Africa or South America (accounts vary) by the well-travelled John Trudgeon. Keeping his chest high and the rest of his body flat, he swung his arms alternately over the water and made a breaststroke or scissor kick with each alternate arm pull. The technique quickly reduced the 100 yards record from 70 to 60 seconds.

Birth of the Crawl

The next big breakthrough came from the Cavill family, a swimming dynasty headed by Englishman Frederick, who emigrated to Australia, where he built pools and taught swimming. All six of his sons became swimming champions and one of them, Dick, made a critical adaptation to the trudgeon after noticing that native swimmers in the South Seas used not only both arms over the water but an up-and-down leg movement. Back in England in 1902, he lowered the 100 yards record to 58.6 seconds and likened his action to 'crawling' through the water. The term frontcrawl was born and the stroke remains the fastest to this day.

Olympic Games swimmers

Although there were no swimming events in the ancient Greek Olympic Games, the sport was one of the nine founding disciplines at the first modern Games and has been a fundamental feature of the programme ever since.

Into the Olympic Games Era

Six events were planned for the first modern Olympiad in 1896 but only four took place – the 100m, 500m and 1200m Freestyle, and the '100m for sailors'. The Hungarian Alfred Hajos's time of 1min 22.20sec in the main 100m event made him the first Olympic swimming champion and began a Hungarian love affair with the sport that survives to this day. He also won the 1200m.

The swimmers used single-arm sidestroke in Athens 1896 but, by the Paris 1900 Olympic Games, double overarm had become the fastest sprint stroke. Backstroke and a team race also made their debuts in a programme that included three freestyle races, an obstacle race, an underwater race and water polo.

Breaststroke entered the Olympic fray for the first time in St Louis in 1904. It joined six freestyle distances ranging from 50 yards to a mile, the 100 yards Backstroke, the 4 x 50 yards Freestyle Relay and the plunge, in which competitors glided as far as they could without using any kind of stroke.

The Birth of Modern Swimming

For the sport of swimming, the launch of world governing body FINA was the most historic moment of the London 1908 Games. Women made their first appearance as Olympic swimmers at the Stockholm 1912 Games, but were restricted to freestyle races. Stockholm also saw the great Hawaiian Duke Kahanamoku win the first of his gold

Dawn Fraser AO, MBE

Victories in the 100m Freestyle in 1956, 1960 and 1964 made Australia's Dawn Fraser the first swimmer to win the same Olympic swimming title three times. Fraser was also the first woman to break the 60-second barrier, later reducing her world record to 58.9, which stood until 1973. Even more remarkably, her 1964 title defence followed a car crash that killed her mother and left her with a fractured cervical vertebra. But she was never far from controversy, most famously at the Tokyo 1964 Games, when she allegedly swam a moat to steal a flag from Emperor Hirohito's Palace.

Mark Spitz

Before the Mexico City 1968 Olympic Games, Mark Spitz of the USA rashly predicted that he would win six gold medals. In fact he won only two – and both of those were in relays. In Munich four years later, sporting the iconic moustache that became his trademark, he put things right in some style, becoming the first athlete in any sport to win seven golds in a single Olympic Games. Three of those wins came in relays, the rest in the 100m and 200m Freestyle and 100m and 200m Butterfly, for each of which he also held the world records for several years.

medals using a frontcrawl style learned from fellow islanders.

Kahanamoku was the first of a generation of Hollywood swimming stars, the most famous of whom was Johnny Weissmuller. The American is best remembered today for his title role in the Tarzan films, but he made his name as the greatest male swimmer of the 1920s, winning five Olympic medals, setting world records in 67 events and never losing a race in his 10-year career. Despite his size, Weissmuller was unusually graceful in the water and swam with his head high, his back slightly arched and a loose, powerful six-beat kick.

An innovation at the Berlin 1936 Games was the use by a few breaststrokers of arms thrown forward above the water in the recovery phase rather than below it. This was clearly faster, but it remained a variation of breaststroke until a year after the Helsinki 1952 Games, when the fourth Olympic stroke was officially born – the butterfly. It first featured in the programme in 1956 in Melbourne, an Olympic Games that also saw the first flip-turn, forerunner of the tumble-turn.

Swimming Superstars

The greatest woman swimmer of the post war years was Australia's Dawn Fraser, whose 100m Freestyle victories in 1956, 1960 and 1964 made her the first swimmer to win the same event at three consecutive Olympic Games.

In Munich in 1972, the freestyler Mark Spitz became the first athlete in any sport to win seven Olympic medals in an Olympic Games. This record was eclipsed in 2008, when his fellow American Michael Phelps won eight golds in Beijing, adding to the four he had won at Athens 2004.

A memorable landmark was the breaking of the 50-second barrier for the Men's 100m Freestyle. The honour fell to Jim Montgomery of the USA, who won the gold medal at the Montreal 1976 Olympic Games in a time of 49.99 seconds.

Training

It is important to know that the effort you invest in training is directly related to the payback in a race. But training is not just about fitness – good technique is just as important.

Joining a club

There is no limit to the number of clubs you can join, although some may insist that you compete for them rather than for their rivals in certain events. To find out which clubs are operating in your area, inquire at your local pool or search the internet.

The Principles of Training

Talk to 100 coaches and you'll probably find 100 different coaching permutations. No two swimmers are the same and no two coaches think exactly the same. But there are some basic principles that can be applied to and adapted for everyone.

During World War II, Tom Delorme, an American orthopaedic surgeon, developed a training system to aid the rapid rehabilitation of soldiers. Known as 'progressive overload', it has since become a fundamental principle of training in many sports, including swimming. It involves the gradual increase in the level of stress placed on the body, which in turn stimulates the body to develop a gradual increase in strength. Muscles, bones, ligaments, tendons, cartilage, blood flow and even nerve connections between the brain and the muscles all benefit from being progressively overloaded. But you also need to build up gradually: too much too soon increases the risk of injury and reduces the effectiveness of the training.

In planning a programme of progressive overload, a coach needs to find a suitable blend of volume and intensity to meet the targets of an individual or a group of swimmers. Distance swimmers will tend to have a greater proportion of aerobic training and cover greater distances. But aerobic work still has an important place in the training plan of the sprinter, providing a fitness platform on which to build.

Recent Training Developments

In recent years there has been a drift away from the very high volumes of aerobic work favoured in the 1990s, when some top swimmers were covering more than 100,000 metres a week. The two-year bodysuit era, which ended on 31 December 2009, has helped to focus more

Joining one of the United Kingdom's 1,400 clubs is a fantastic way of becoming involved in swimming.

attention on technique, streamlining and body shape.

Traditionally, coaches and swimmers work on endurance first and gradually build the intensity as the season progresses. A radical development since 2004, however, is 'reverse periodisation' of training, which emphasises speed in the early part of the season and adds endurance work later. This theory was developed by Australian coach Shannon Rollason, who advocates improving speed while the body is fresh. Two of his female swimmers won gold in the Athens 2004 Olympic Games, but the approach is so far only proven with out-and-out sprinters in the 50m and 100m events.

Clothing – swimsuits

The last few years have seen a revolution in the field of swimming costumes – followed by some major backtracking by the swimming authorities as technological advances got out of hand.

Hi-tech Advances

Between February 2008 and the end of December 2009, more than 250 world records were broken – many times the number that would normally be expected to fall in a two-year period. The undisputed reason for this dramatic rise in standards was the rapid advances in swimsuit technology. Manufacturers spent vast sums developing swimsuits that covered most of the body, with a polyurethane rather than textile content that ranged from 50 to 100 per cent. The suits were also designed to strategically compress the body in order to improve streamlining and body shape, aid muscle performance and reduce fatigue. Some suits were reckoned to produce benefits that would take weeks to achieve through training in a gym.

Human Power Only

Following a series of crisis meetings in 2009, the sport began 2010 with a new and complex set of costume rules. Now male costumes must not extend above the navel or below the knee while women's costumes must not cover the neck or extend beyond the shoulders or below the knee. Material must be 'textile fabric' and not coated by anything affecting its 'open mesh structure'. Costumes must have a maximum thickness of 0.8 millimetres and a buoyancy effect not greater than 0.5 Newton. Material must have a defined level of permeability with no zippers or fastening system. Features that provide external stimulation, such as pain reduction, chemical release and electro-stimulation, are banned.

The effects of the rule change were immediate. In the first eight months of 2010, not a single world record – and only one European record – was broken. But at least the swimming community knew that the times recorded owed more to the talent and training of the athletes than it did to the design of their costumes.

Competing swimmers are required to wear only one swimsuit 'in one or two pieces' (in the high-tech era, some wore two or even three bodysuits on top of each other to amplify the benefits). Costumes must be non-transparent, 'in good moral taste' and not marked with any symbol that could be considered offensive. These last two rules also apply to caps and goggles.

Swimwear manufacturers have amended their costume designs to comply with the rule changes. Beyond that, it's a case of personal choice, although it is clearly an advantage to have a closely fitting rather than a loose costume, to reduce water resistance. A full list of approved costumes can be found on the FINA website fina.org.

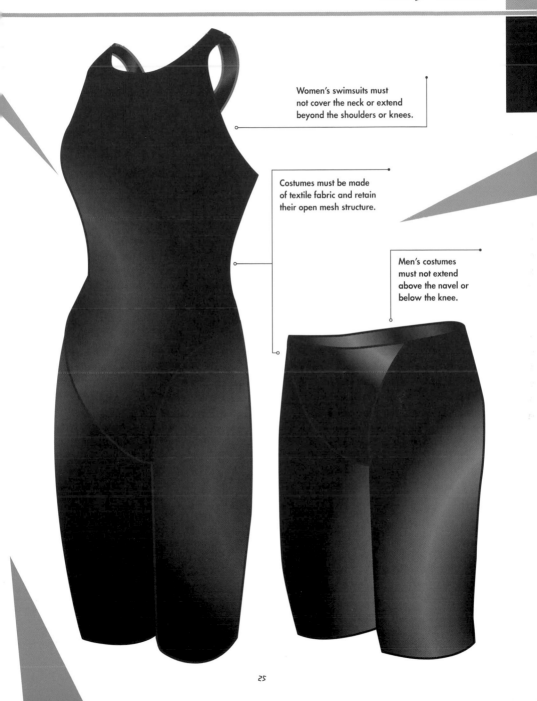

Women's swimsuits must not cover the neck or extend beyond the shoulders or knees.

Costumes must be made of textile fabric and retain their open mesh structure.

Men's costumes must not extend above the navel or below the knee.

Clothing accessories

Over the last 30 or 40 years, goggles have become an essential piece of kit for almost every competitive swimmer and most fitness swimmers. Virtually all female swimmers and a significant number of men also wear swim-hats. Smaller numbers use ear-plugs.

Goggles

The serious swimmer spends hours in the water almost every day and the prolonged exposure to chlorine and other chemicals can cause eye irritation. A well-fitting pair of goggles will prevent this, as well as offering the added bonus of vastly improved visibility in the water. They work by sealing off the water from around the eyes.

Most swimmers like to wear goggles when racing as well as training, although this does come with an element of risk. The most common problem is that the goggles slip during the dive or underwater phase, and end up around your mouth or throat or adrift in the pool. This can be an uncomfortable and disconcerting experience and may affect your performance adversely. Yet stopping to put the goggles back on would cost vital seconds as well as risking disqualification in all except freestyle events.

The risk of losing your goggles can be greatly reduced by wearing them tighter, making sure they are well-suctioned, and diving correctly with the head down and arms cutting into the water first. Many swimmers use different pairs of goggles for training and racing, the former being much looser than the competition set. It's a good idea to carry a spare pair in case the head-strap or bridge breaks as you put them on.

The choice of goggles is a very individual affair and can only be decided by trying them out at training sessions and discovering which brand and design suits you best. Most designs have a rubber seal around the eye-cap but for racing, many swimmers favour Swedish goggles, so-called because

Finding the perfect goggles for you is a matter of trial and error.

they were first developed by a Swedish company. These have a hard rather than a rubber seal.

In open water swimming, the contrast between the warm body and the cold water often causes the goggles to steam up. This can be prevented by spreading saliva around the eye-cup or using an anti-fog spray before you put them on.

There is also a safety issue. Injuries have been caused by the eye-pieces springing back as the user puts them on. This can be avoided by putting the eye-pieces over the eyes first, and only then stretching the rubber strap over the head.

Hats

Some pools insist that swimmers wear hats to protect their filters from clogged hair. But there are also benefits for the swimmer: they provide somewhere to tuck away long hair, protect the hair from chlorine damage and reduce the drag caused by loose hair. Hats are even more important in open water, as they protect the head from the sun and the cold.

Ear-plugs

Ear-plugs come in various designs and will help to prevent problems caused by prolonged exposure to chlorine, which can be a problem for swimmers with particularly sensitive ears. The modern range includes 'putty' plugs, which cost only a few pounds and can be moulded into the ear before every swim. Plugs can also be custom-made for the individual ear.

Ear-plugs come in a wide range of designs.

Hats protect the hair from chlorine damage.

Training aids

The modern swimmer turns up at the pool with a great deal more than the traditional costume, hat and goggles. Visit any club session and at the end of each lane you'll see a veritable mountain of training aids – tools that are used to isolate specific aspects of training or stroke technique.

Kickboard

Along with pull-buoy, hand-paddles and fins, the kickboard is a staple ingredient of every serious swimmer's armoury. The board is held at arm's length to stabilise the forward part of the body as the swimmer propels himself by frontcrawl or breaststroke kicking. By isolating the leg-kick, swimmers can work at a higher intensity to create an overload effect that will increase the power and endurance of the swimmer's leg action. As well as a conditioning tool, isolated kicking can also be used to improve technique. Some people use kickboards in backstroke but this is hardly necessary, as the arms can be extended beyond the head or by sculling at the sides. Using a board for dolphin kicking for butterfly is not advisable, as it puts too much stress on the back.

Pull-buoy

The pull-buoy is an hourglass-shaped float that is held between the thighs to support the body's centre of gravity while the swimmer works on arm-pull. With a pull-buoy in place, the body position is raised slightly and water resistance reduced. This in turn reduces fatigue, enabling swimmers to increase their volume of work as they practise their arm skills.

Fins

Flippers are known in the swimming community as fins. They come in various shapes and sizes and can be used for different purposes. Short-bladed fins, which have become particularly fashionable in recent years, are used for high-intensity kick work. Their design enables the swimmer to increase the power and speed of their kicking – but

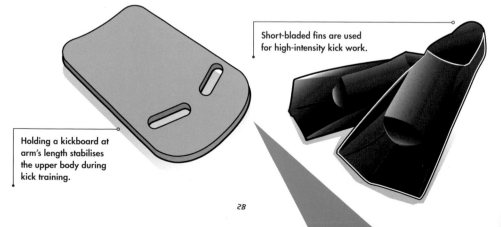

Short-bladed fins are used for high-intensity kick work.

Holding a kickboard at arm's length stabilises the upper body during kick training.

they also have to work very hard for it, thus creating another overload situation. Fins also aid ankle flexibility.

Larger fins have slipped out of fashion but are still useful for lower-intensity work. They are normally used for underwater kicking, as they help swimmers to improve their streamlining and maximise distance during the transitional kicking phase that follows the start and turn in a race. Because swimmers travel faster underwater than on the surface, maximising speed and improving streamlining underwater is clearly a useful skill. So while short fins are used for overloading, long fins fulfil an almost opposite purpose.

A third type of fin is the monofin, which first appeared in the USSR in 1972. Monofins are primarily used in free-swimming and fin-swimming, but some competitive swimmers use them to develop the power of their butterfly kick.

Traditionally, fins have not been used for breaststroke, their designs being unsuitable for the frog-like kick action. In recent years, however, manufacturers have come up with the 'positive drive fin' or PDF, which has been found to be suitable for breaststroke as well as other kicks.

Paddles

Hand-paddles are another overload tool, designed to strengthen the arm-pull by making the swimmer employ greater power than they could exert with bare hands. Wearing paddles while

swimming with the same stroke rate and length for a race will increase both your power and speed.

Finger-paddles can be used for sculling on all strokes but are particularly popular with breaststrokers, as they help to maintain a feel for the water and to strengthen the pull while also reducing the risk of tendonitis and other overload injuries.

Snorkels

A growing number of swimmers are adding snorkels to their kit bag. They use the snorkel during frontcrawl training in order to maintain a streamlined position on the water surface. Repeatedly rehearsing the optimum body position encourages the swimmer to maintain a similar position when racing.

Hand-paddles are an overload tool designed to strengthen the pull.

Finger-paddles are particularly popular with breaststrokers.

Training aids

Stroke-rate monitors, swim benches and personal lap pools are among the more sophisticated training aids now available – but you may need a plumber, an electrician and a carpenter to install certain types of lap pool.

Stroke-rate Monitor

A stroke-rate monitor is designed to help swimmers rehearse the way in which they intend to swim a race. By emitting a 'beep' into the ears, it helps swimmers to adopt a specific stroke rate and speed for each section of the race – which may vary, of course, especially over longer distances.

The traditional way of measuring your heart rate during the rest spells in a training set is to place your finger on the carotid artery in the neck, count the beats over six seconds and multiply by ten to ascertain the rate per minute. However, some swimmers use a heart-rate monitor to obtain a more accurate reading. The traditionally recommended maximum heart rate is 220 beats per minute less the swimmer's age – so the MHR of a 50-year-old, for example, would be 220 minus 50 = 170bpm. But individuals vary enormously.

Resistance Tools

Drag shorts are a costume addition and another overload tool. They are worn over the costume to increase water resistance while also maintaining a normal body position.

Other resistance tools include bungee belts and stretch cords, which enable swimmers to pull while tethered; drag rings to hold the ankles together and increase drag; and drag belts, which are designed to increase drag and thus improve strength and power by catching water in cups attached to a belt around the waist.

The swim bench is used to practise stroke movements out of the water and correct flaws.

Drag shorts are worn over the costume to increase water resistance in training.

Top-range Training Aids

The swim bench is a more sophisticated (and more expensive) item of dry-land apparatus that is often seen on the poolside, but can also be used at home – though not all coaches choose to use them. As a tool to improve technique, it is used to practise stroke movements out of the water and correct flaws, such as dropped elbows and incomplete finishing or follow-through of the stroke. It can also be used as a conditioning tool to build strength, power and endurance.

For those with a spare room or some space in the garden, the ultimate training aid is a personal lap pool – especially one with an adjustable current that enables you to swim as long as you wish without ever reaching the pool's end. A hydraulic motor powers a continuous loop of water, which the swimmer can set to their own pace.

Training safety

Swimming carries a lower risk of injury than most sports and those risks can be reduced even further by various means, such as sensible and educated coaching in the early years, development of core stability, thorough warm-ups and good stroke technique.

Mix It Up

One of the strongest recommendations from the Amateur Swimming Association (ASA) and British Swimming is to avoid stroke specialisation at too young an age. In fact, for 'age group' swimmers (which are defined as girls aged 13 and under and boys aged 14 and under) the advice is to base the training on an individual medley programme, which embraces all four strokes. Specialist sprint training and excessive metreage are also to be avoided at this stage.

According to coach Paul Hogg, 'too much of one stroke too early leads to injuries. If coaches, swimmers and parents become too fixated on their best stroke and the swimmers have to do a lot more of it when they are only 11 or so, they will start to stagnate physically and mentally.'

There is also a strong emphasis on good core stability (see page 58), which will not only improve streamlining and help the arms and legs to work more efficiently, but reduce the risk of injury. As in any sport, a thorough warm-up before strenuous exercise is also important for injury prevention.

Avoiding Injury and Over-training

If you are suffering from an injury or illness and are unsure how to respond, seek advice from an expert. Your coach should certainly be informed, but you may also need to see a doctor, physiotherapist or other practitioner. Training with an injury or illness may only make matters worse, although much depends on the nature of the problem. Some lesser injuries can benefit from relatively gentle exercise, as it gets the blood circulating, activates self-healing processes and keeps the muscles active. But that's something only

A swimmer with a serious shoulder injury will sometimes train only on kick until the problem recedes.

you and the experts can judge.

Over-training is another danger, although it is often confused with simple fatigue. Chris Nesbit, England's head coach at the 2010 Commonwealth Games, explains: 'People use the term "over-trained" when they really mean "over-tired". Over-training is usually associated with people doing too much volume and intensity of training – although a training volume that may suit one swimmer may not suit another. When you are over-trained, you can't even swim what would previously have been mediocre times. Over-training is a serious situation and not one you are going to recover from overnight. It may take months and months to rectify, whereas if you are just fatigued you may simply need a few days' rest or a change in the mode of training.'

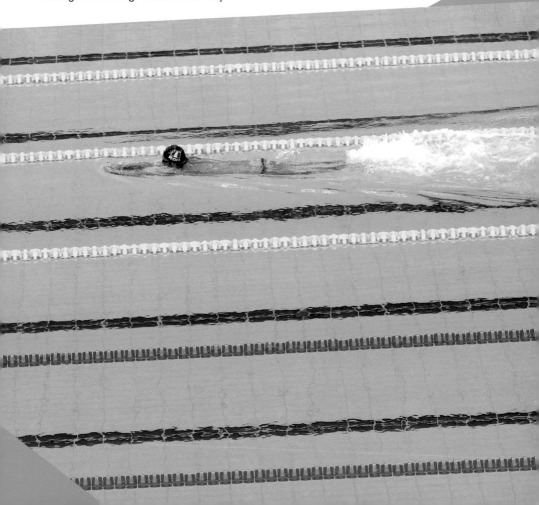

What do you want to achieve?

Not everyone is going to be an Olympic Games swimmer or even a national champion. But we can all set targets for ourselves in any area of life – and setting goals and then working towards them makes it more likely that we will achieve them.

Setting Goals

Whatever activity you are pursuing, goal-setting will provide you with a focus for the journey ahead and for the strategy you adopt to reach your destination.

There's nothing wrong with having ambition or having a dream. They provide the inspiration to make plans and progress and get things done. But dreams also need to be realistic. By all means dream about being an Olympic swimmer, an Olympic champion even – but if you are not already an international swimmer, there may be a few lesser hurdles to overcome first. Set goals that are challenging but achievable. And set goals to achieve as stepping-stones towards the final goal.

Exactly where you should pitch your goals depends partly on your age, ability and present level of performance. Improving your personal-best time can be a goal for everyone. If you are just setting out, your early targets could include getting into your club's team in the local league, winning your events at the club championships or qualifying for the county championships. Beyond that, regional and national championships await. If you're already established at national or international level, the Olympic Games may already be a realistic goal.

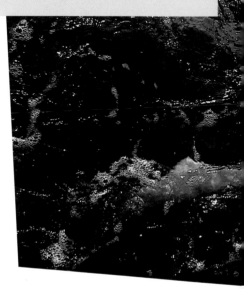

Assessing Your Progress

At the highest level, long-term goal-setting can extend over a number of seasons. International coaches usually work to a four-year cycle, which is designed to peak at the Olympic Games. Along the way, they will set a number of short-term and medium-term goals involving other major competitions, such as European and world championships, all of which are seen as steps on the road towards the ultimate target. From time to time, coach and swimmer will need to consider their progress so far, and whether their goals need to be revised or adjusted.

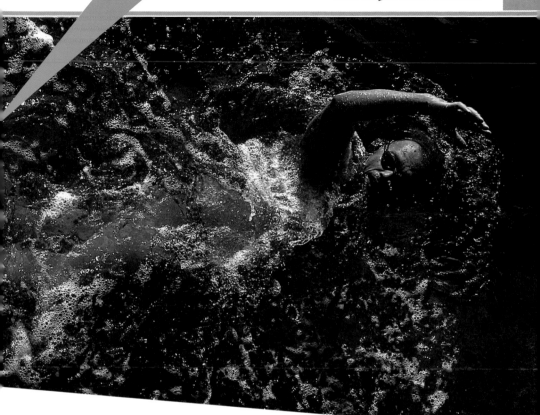

An important part of setting goals is to prepare a strategy to achieve them – and that may involve more than just a training plan, vital though that is. Lifestyle goal-setting may also be important. 'For a young age-group swimmer, it could be as simple as coming to five training sessions a week instead of four,' says coach Chris Nesbit. 'It may involve focusing on one point in each session and trying to do that well. It may be about getting enough sleep or rest, about having positive distractions away from

Goals need to be challenging but also realistic.

the pool – work, studies, leisure. It may be about having nutritional goals. Does he need to put on weight or lose weight? Is he getting enough protein? Is he eating too much carbohydrate? It could be that someone has great physical potential but a negative attitude. It could be a goal to change that. You don't see negative swimmers on the podium.'

Training plan

To train effectively, you need a plan – and the starting point in drawing up any training plan is identifying the big competition that is your ultimate goal. There may be interim goals but they are also stepping-stones to the big one.

Working in Cycles

Coaches work in cycles. At the highest level, swimmers will usually work to a four-year cycle that aims to peak at the Olympic Games. At lower levels most swimmers work to a yearly cycle leading up to their main target for the year – say, the county, regional or national championships. Within that yearly cycle, there may be three 'macrocycles', typically covering the periods September to December, January to March and March to the summer championships in July or August. An eighteen-week macrocycle could be broken into, for example, three six-week 'mesocycles', and these in turn into three one-week 'microcycles'. 'That's when you work on a certain energy system or do a certain type of work on each day so that it all links in together,' says Paul Hogg, a leading coach. 'At the end of each microcycle you would have a competition to gauge where your swimmers are as you go through the season.'

Keeping Track

Closely linked to the training plan is the swimmer's personal logbook. You can buy a logbook from the ASA or just use a lined notebook to keep a record of training sessions,

competitions, pulse rate, weight, height, sleep and any health or other issues.

'Swimmers should take their resting pulse rate when they wake up every morning and if it goes ten beats per minute above their normal level it can be a warning sign that they are getting worn down, or that there's an illness,' says Hogg.

'Weight and height should be measured once a week. It's a delicate area but if a swimmer has had a big increase or loss in weight you need to look for the cause. It may be just that they've had a growth spurt, but it may be there's a problem relating to training or diet that needs to be monitored. Sleep is very important. That's when they recover. If you have to get up early you need to go to bed early.'

Noting details of training sessions – including distances, strokes, stroke counts and times – and also of competitions can identify trends in performance. Hogg asks his swimmers to comment on how they felt during each training session and what they improved during it. 'Why go

to a pool for two hours and not improve on something?' he says. 'Even if they haven't had a great session and haven't hit their target times, they can usually find something they have improved. It's important to come out of a session saying they have achieved something. I look at the logbooks each week and comment on what they have done really well and what they need to focus on next week.'

Top swimmers usually work to a four-year cycle that aims to peak at the Olympic Games.

Basic training

Coach Paul Hogg compares training to building a house: 'If you don't build a solid foundation, somewhere along the line the house will collapse. In swimming, the foundations are endurance and stamina. If that base isn't good enough, you will dip into your other energy systems far more quickly.'

Traditionally, coaches start a training cycle with a block of aerobic training to build an endurance platform for the season to come. In technical terms, aerobic training is designed to improve the absorption and transportation of oxygen through the body. By swimming at a sustained and relatively steady pace over longer distances, the supply of oxygen is able to keep pace with the body's demand for it. Sprinting, on the other hand, is anaerobic, which means its demand for oxygen outstrips the supply, and the pace can only be sustained for a limited time. Coaches talk about anaerobic swimming 'incurring an oxygen debt'; aerobic training is debt-free.

Paul Hogg has a second analogy to describe the purpose of endurance training. 'It's a bit like putting a deposit in the bank,' he says. 'You are putting money into your account so that when you come to make a withdrawal – in a race – you have a bigger deposit to withdraw from before you go into your overdraft towards the end of your race.'

Typical training sets during this low-intensity 'aerobic 1' period would be 10 x 400m or 5 x 800m with a fixed rest of, say, 5 to 30 seconds between each 400 or 800m. In heart-rate terms, swimmers will be working at 50 to 60 beats per minute below their maximum. An individual's maximum heart rate can be determined by a specific test set in training – but the coach needs to be sure that the swimmer is fully rested and not fatigued or unwell when the test is done. Sprinters will have a different test-set from those specialising in 200m or above. An individual's maximum heart rate will also differ from one sport to another.

To reduce the risk of boredom, many coaches will mix the strokes during training (alternating 200m freestyle and 200m individual medley, for example) or introduce other challenges, such as holding or reducing the stroke count or pushing a specific distance off the wall at each turn. Variety is vital in any training schedule. Simply swimming up and down can be boring but the variety of strokes, distances and drills in a session that is well thought-out will help to maintain interest. It's also important to maintain good technique on every stroke however tired you get. If you can hold your stroke in training, you'll stand a better chance of holding it in a race, when the pressure is really on.

Endurance sets in the early season create a fitness platform on which to build.

Increasing the intensity

Low-intensity training will provide an endurance base on which a swimmer can build as the season progresses. The intensity will gradually increase to reach a peak a few days or a couple of weeks before the big competition, from which point the training will be systematically tapered.

Building Your Aerobic Capability

'Aerobic 2' is classed as 'aerobic maintenance' and will involve repeated distances ranging from 200 metres to 1,500m. In heart-rate terms, aerobic maintenance is 40 to 50 beats below maximum. This phase is followed by 'aerobic 3' or 'aerobic development', with a heart-rate target of 30 to 40 beats below maximum.

As the intensity continues to build, you will move into anaerobic threshold work – the point where lactate accumulation begins to rise sharply. For a national-standard youth swimmer (girls aged 14+, boys 15+), a typical quality endurance intensity set might be 30 x 100m on 1min 20secs with a heart rate of 20 to 30 beats below maximum. If the swimmer can complete each 100m in 65 to 68 seconds, it will provide 12 to 15 seconds rest between each repeat.

The most intensive training phase involves critical speed (which some coaches call 'heart-rate sets') and a heart rate of 10 to 20 beats below maximum. Typical sets might be 24 or 30 x 100m; or 1 x 200m, 2 x 100m and 4 x 50m repeated four times to give a total of 2,400m. Most coaches recommend a maximum of 30 minutes for a set of this intensity. 'A swimmer who can hit 60 seconds per 100m and 20 beats below max can do 30 x 100m in 30 minutes of actual swimming time,' says Paul Hogg. 'But if critical speed is 1min 10secs, you won't do 30 x 100m in 30 minutes.'

Preparing for Competition

As the targeted competition approaches, training distances should be gradually reduced and work on starts, turns and sprints increased to sharpen the mind and body for the challenge to come. The ideal taper can range from two or three days for one swimmer to two or three weeks or even more for another. Trial and error is the only way to identify what suits each individual.

Some sprinters now use 'reverse periodisation', which reverses the traditional training plan by working on speed development early in the season. 'After that they go into a lactate production phase so the body learns how to start producing lactate,' says Hogg. 'Then it goes into a phase where it learns how to tolerate the lactate that builds up during the hard work. Then there's a lactate removal phase to teach the body how to flush lactate out efficiently. Finally you move into a race preparation period and then into a taper.'

A good training regime will prepare the swimmer to peak at their targeted competition.

Avoiding Over-competing

A danger facing young swimmers is the temptation to compete too often. The Long Term Athlete Development Model is a commonly adopted framework which supports the development of young swimmers. It provides a guide to optimal performance and a planning tool based on scientific research. British Swimming recommends no more than about twelve competitions a year – that is once a month on average. Because swimmers like to swim fast in every competition, there is a temptation to ease back the training for a couple of days beforehand - but such mini-tapers will also reduce the benefits of the greater training regime.

Stroke Drills

Many coached sessions include drills designed to correct faults in the stroke or prevent them developing. There are many to choose from but for frontcrawl a popular drill is 'finger-drag' in which the fingers tickle the water surface during the recovery phase to keep the elbows high; for backstroke, 'double-arm' encourages a good hand entry position; for butterfly, a right-arm left-arm double-arm sequence is popular; and for breaststroke, two kicks followed by one pull or vice-versa.

Warming up

There are two aspects to warming up in swimming – land exercises at poolside, followed by a swimming warm-up in the pool. The main aim is to increase the muscle temperature as preparation for the activity that is about to take place – both in training and in competition.

Poolside Warm-up

'You are also looking at the neuro-muscular co-ordination,' says Pat Dunleavy, formerly head physiotherapist with the Great Britain swim team. 'If you get out of the car and get straight in the pool and do a hard set, you are not going to produce as good an effect as you would if you do a warm-up. Your body is not going to be prepared for the activity. If you don't warm up, you are really preparing to fail rather than to perform.'

In a team situation, there's an additional reason for dry-land warm-up exercises – team-building. 'You can build camaraderie and the mental focus with coaches supporting the athletes. Peer pressure drives it forward,' Dunleavy adds.

Land exercises include skipping with a rope, jogging on the spot, burpees, small tuck-jumps and lunge walking. Squats are also recommended, gradually increasing the range of motion. A good stretching exercise that doubles as a rehearsal for the race start involves stretching into a streamlined position with arms and hands fully extended above the head, then bringing them down to the diving start position. The sequence can be repeated three or four times, gradually increasing the range.

Dunleavy recommends 10–15 minutes of dry-land warm-up exercises on the poolside. 'If you are part of a team, you can easily start to lose your focus if you spend 30 or 40 minutes warming up,' he says. 'You want to keep them focused and alert.' If individual swimmers want to do more routines afterwards, they can.

Water Warm-up

The greater part of the warm-up, however, is usually done in the pool. In training this will be done as the opening set of the session. Before a competition, most swimmers will benefit from a lengthy warm-up that includes some work probably at race pace, though not usually over the race distance. At international level, warm-ups usually range from under 1,500 metres to over 3,000m. At local level there may not be the time or pool space for this, but it is important to warm up adequately and use the time you have productively.

The pool warm-up is also an opportunity to rehearse turns and familiarise yourself with the characteristics of the pool, such as the surface and the markings on the turning walls. Some walls are more slippery than others.

Sprint Warm-up

Many competitions will offer one or two dedicated sprint lanes towards the end of each warm-up session. These provide an opportunity to practise your start, try out your race pace for a few strokes and check that your goggles are tight enough to stay on when you dive. It is not necessary to swim the whole length – but don't turn round and swim back, as sprint lanes are one-way-traffic!

Squats (left) and walking lunges are useful warm-up exercises, though you won't need the dumbbells on poolside.

Begin a tuck jump with arms outstretched and come down into a flat-foot squat.

With arms still parallel to the floor, bring up the knees as close as possible to the chest.

Come up on to your toes and jump in the air.

Warming down

Warming down after a competition or a high-intensity training session is almost as important as warming up. Power exercises, especially sprinting, when the rate of demand for energy is high, cause a build-up of lactate in the muscles, and swimming-down is needed to assist its removal.

Lactate Build-up

Lactate concentration is not a bad thing. It's actually beneficial and ensures that energy production is maintained and exercise can continue. But during high intensity work, the lactate is produced faster than the tissues can remove it and a build-up occurs. If it is then allowed to linger in the system, it can reduce the body's recovery efficiency and may contribute to delayed muscle soreness or stiffness. This in turn could adversely affect a further performance taking place later that day or the following day. The aim of the warm-down is to return the body to a balanced state as close as possible to what it was before the race, so you are able to race again at maximum capacity.

In the Pool

Research shows that the majority of the warm-down is best done in the pool rather than on land. But it's a fallacy to think that a few lengths of gentle swimming will do the job. It almost certainly won't. Evidence suggests that a more effective warm-down will start at a faster pace and ease off gradually. It will also feature a higher proportion of kicks, as the legs harbour more than their share of lactate.

How long the warm-down should last varies from swimmer to swimmer. At the highest level, some sprinters will use a quality, well-planned warm-down of 600 metres to 800m. Others may need as much as 1,000m or even more. Distance swimmers may require less but generally like to do over 1,500m.

Out of the Pool

In lower levels of competition, a warm-down of such duration may be a luxury that is not available to them. Some pools have no warm-down facility available, or perhaps only a shallow, over-crowded learner pool. In these cases, swimmers can go some way to dissipating the lactate by doing some light land activity such as walking, arm movements or gentle skipping.

There are several other ways to help clean up the lactate. Many international teams include physiotherapists whose role is not just to treat injuries, but also to use massage to help swimmers to warm down more effectively. A rub or massage is not, of course, usually available to the average club swimmer, although freelance physiotherapists can sometimes be found offering their services at national competitions.

A handy hint available to every swimmer is to lie on your back on a bed or floor with your feet against the wall at a higher level than your body. Doing

Burpees begin from a standing position coming down to a squat with hands on the floor.

Jump the feet back so that the body is straight, then jump back to the previous position and up to the vertical with arms above the head.

Gentle jogging on the spot can be used as a warm up or warm-down exercise if no warm-down pool is available.

Skipping is another activity that some swimmers use to warm up or warm down.

this for ten to fifteen minutes three or four times in the afternoon or evening after racing will assist the body's recovery rate and aid lactate absorption.

In addition, some athletes wear compression garments that are designed to help the circulation to rid itself of waste products when the muscles aren't working.

45

Diet and hydration

You wouldn't expect a car to work properly without the right kind of fuel in the petrol tank. Likewise, you can't expect your body to work to its full potential if you don't keep it suitably fuelled and well-watered.

Competitive swimmers train long and hard but without the right nutrition and hydration, they are not making the most of that training. They will also be more susceptible to illness, injury and fatigue.

Staying Hydrated

Dehydration is an enemy of every athlete: the loss of just 2 per cent of bodyweight leads to a big drop-off in performance. It may not seem like it but you can sweat just as much while swimming as you would during land exercise. In a single training session, you could lose as much as a kilo of bodyweight. Put another way, that's a litre of sweat. Hanging around a hot, steamy poolside for hours during a competition can also lead to dehydration.

You can tell if you're dehydrated from the colour of your urine – the darker the shade of yellow, the more dehydrated you are. You can even get a colour chart to help your assessment! You'll also sweat and urinate less when dehydrated.

To maintain your fluid levels, take an ample supply of drink to every training session and competition. It can be water, perhaps with a splash of squash added for flavour and a pinch of salt to replace the sodium that is lost when you sweat. You can also buy a sports drink

that will give you an additional source of carbohydrate, as well as liquid. Carbohydrates in liquid form give you energy and can be used when it's not convenient to eat solid food.

Eating Right

For optimum health and performance, a balanced and varied diet is essential. A balanced diet will include:
- at least five portions of fruit a day;
- carbohydrates, such as cereals and bread (preferably wholegrain), potatoes, wholewheat pasta and brown rice, which should make up 50 to 70 per cent of a swimmer's diet;
- meat, fish, beans or other protein alternatives;
- two to three portions of milk or other dairy products daily;
- foods containing essential fats – swimmers should take 15 to 30 per cent of their energy from high-fat foods, such as avocadoes, eggs and olives. Up to 10 per cent of the fat content should be saturated.

Consultant-nutritionist and Amateur Swimming Association adviser Martin MacDonald suggests a high-carbohydrate meal two to four hours before swimming (though not in the morning, of course!) and cereals, yoghurts, fruit, fruit juice or milkshakes an hour before. The last thing you need before training or a competition is a traditional English fry-up, which will lay heavily in the stomach for hours.

Recovery Food and Drink

Immediately after the swim, MacDonald recommends milkshakes, yoghurt drinks, fruit smoothies made with milk and sandwiches with lean meat. And

an hour after, it's important to have a meal that includes protein, such as lean meat or fish, as well as potatoes, vegetables and rice or pasta. On a competition day, this will need to be adjusted to fit in with your programme of events.

Taking on liquid carbohydrates is even more important for long-distance swimming in open water.

The mental edge

Even Olympic champions have bad days as well as good ones. It's how we deal with them that matters. Setbacks are there to be overcome, nerves and pressure to be used in a positive way. Mental toughness is an essential skill for the competitive swimmer.

Developing Mental Toughness

Sports psychologists talk about the 'four Cs' – the four elements that underpin mental toughness: Concentration, Confidence, Commitment and Control.

Concentration is the ability to stay focused. Life is full of distractions and when you get to a big competition they will confront you at every turn. During a training phase, you need to keep your eye on the ball and focus on the task in hand. When you get to the competition, focus on your performance and don't be distracted by all the things going on around you. Anything less and you will not maximise your swimming ability. Some people concentrate better than others, but it's a skill that can be developed.

Confidence is fundamental to success in any sport. It's linked to goal-setting – achieving your short-term and medium-term goals will help to build your belief in your own ability. Thoughts of defeat or failure, on the other hand, will have a detrimental effect.

Commitment is about mental drive – the will to win. Modern sport demands a great deal from its participants, especially swimmers, who invest huge amounts of time in training. By any standards, that's a big commitment with the potential to impact on other areas of their lives, such as studies and social life. But you can't succeed without it.

Control is about controlling your emotions and dealing with stress and anxiety. Sport is a stressful business and everyone suffers from nerves at some point. The key is to harness the adrenalin and use it positively. 'Pressure is your friend, not your enemy,' says Dr Ian Maynard, Professor of Sport Psychology at Sheffield Hallam University. 'Your body wants butterflies because that's what gives you the edge. But you need to have your butterflies flying in formation – to use them positively and drive in the right direction.'

Dealing with Adversity

Dealing with the downs can be the biggest challenge. Most young swimmers reach a stage in their careers when their times are standing still or even going backwards. Everyone has failures as well as successes. It can be disappointing, even depressing. But again, that's where mental toughness comes in.

'A mentally tough person deals with it,' says Dr Maynard. 'The great athlete uses it in the right way. It drives them forward. You learn from the bad days and take them with you. You pick out the positive and you don't make the same mistake. People who get to the top are driven by a need to achieve rather than a fear of failure.'

Achieving short- and medium-turn goals helps to build belief in your own ability.

Land training

While the pool should be the main focus for training, land work is also a vital ingredient of the serious swimmer's training. 'You can work on natural ability in the water for so long but eventually you will hit a plateau. Everybody does,' says land coach Bronwin Carter.

Training Appropriately

Strength, power, core strength and flexibility can all be improved by various kinds of land training, which now forms a regular and in some cases daily part of training programmes. An adult male sprinter may spend as much as 50 per cent of his training time in the gym, though that is the extreme end of the spectrum. But if it's not done properly, land training also carries a greater risk of injury. As with any form of exercise, warming up is essential to reduce the risk of pulled muscles. So is correct technique. Some clubs have their swimmers screened by a physiotherapist for physical strengths and weaknesses to help avoid injury. Then they work to turn the weaknesses into strengths.

Training with Weights

It's also important that young swimmers are not introduced to weight load resistance training too young and around 15 years old is considered about the right age for young swimmers to learn the basic techniques. Again, correct technique is vital to avoid injury. Weight-room exercises that are suitable for swimmers include cleans and snatches, reactive squats, reactive bench, small weights, small dumbbells and kettle-bells. Some exercises apply to all strokes, but some are stroke-specific.

Complementary Exercises

At one leading club, where swimmers are encouraged to do up to an hour's land training before every swimming session if their personal timetables permit, children aged about 11 and younger are given a form of circuit training. 'At that age they love to run so we give them small hurdles, ladders and that sort of work to enhance their fitness,' says Carter. 'When they get a bit older we go through a series of exercises using medicine ball and core work.'

Flexibility exercises should feature in every swimmer's land-training programme.

An increasing number of coaches are advising their swimmers to do Pilates to improve both stability in the water and muscle-efficiency (see page 58), and yoga to increase their flexibility.

Land training should also be regarded as complementary to pool training, rather than as a replacement for it. Communication between the swimming coaches and their land-training colleagues is vital to ensure a co-ordinated programme.

Injury prevention

As a non-contact sport performed at fairly low speeds in a relatively weightless environment, swimming has the lowest incidence of injury of any major sport. Problems do occur, of course, but many of them are preventable.

Most swimming injuries fall into one of two categories – those caused by mishaps on the pool-deck or in the water, and those brought about by chronic overuse.

Accidents in the Pool

Tiles on the pool-deck are often slippery and many injuries occur due to people falling over. Many could be avoided by walking rather than running on poolside and by generally taking care. Broken fingers are not uncommon, usually due to people hitting the end-wall of the sprint lane during warm-ups. Goggles can cause injuries to the wearer or people nearby by springing back as they are being put on incorrectly. Again, such problems can be avoided by taking more care. Good lane discipline will also help to avoid collisions in crowded training or warm-up lanes.

Chronic Injuries

The most common injury due to overuse is 'swimmer's shoulder'. A top swimmer today will rotate each shoulder an estimated 1 to 1.5 million times in a year – probably more than most people do in a lifetime. The demands on the body are obvious but medical thinking on this issue has changed in recent years. 'We used to think it was anatomical factors causing the impingement at the shoulder joint, but now it appears it is largely due to muscle weakness and imbalance, as well as biomechanical faults,' says Dr Ian Gordon, head of medical services at the ASA. 'It's essentially an instability of the supporting muscles around the shoulder joint.'

Such problems can be prevented or treated by a combination of stroke correction and core stability exercises. 'If you have subtle problems with your stroke – the angles of your stroke are wrong – you can get chronic problems with your shoulders,' says Dr Gordon. 'So you correct the stroke but, more importantly, you also build up the core muscles. This will minimise the risk of chronic long-term problems. You are using the shoulder a lot whatever stroke you swim. The aim is to keep it supple and keep it stretched but also to increase the core stability of the joint.'

Stroke-specific Injuries

Some problems are associated with particular strokes. The common condition known as 'breaststroker's knee' relates to a weakness of the medial collateral ligament caused by repeated stretching during the outward-turning whip-kick leg action in breaststroke. It can be prevented by improving stroke biomechanics and technique, and treated through a combination of rest and physiotherapy.

'Butterflier's back' is an injury of the lower back resulting from the hyperextension involved in butterfly. In severe cases, it can lead to stress fractures of the pars (part of the vertebra, causing a condition known as spondylolysis or even spondylolisthesis, where one vertebra slips forward on to another). Strengthening the abdominal and back extensor muscles and stretching the hamstring and gluteal muscles will help to prevent the problem. If symptoms do occur, restricted use of the stroke is recommended. The risk of spinal injury can also be reduced by avoiding the dolphin leg-kick stroke when performed with a fixed float.

A top swimmer rotates each shoulder 1 to 1.5 million times in a year.

The basics

Getting the basics right is important in skill acquisition in sport. In swimming, there are a number of factors that can impact on your ability to conquer the basics. Some are fixed, such as body shape and type, but for others, a level of awareness can help to improve your performance.

The science of swimming

Swimming is about generating and maintaining momentum in the water. The key principles, such as balance, timing, buoyancy and the factors which influence propulsion, all relate to generating momentum.

Balance and Propulsion

Balance is influenced by your ability to position your body to reduce all unwanted movements, and by making the body as propulsive as possible. This balance is closely associated with body form, which manifests itself in two ways. First, the position your body either adopts or is forced to adopt by the water as you stroke through or over it. Second, the amount of body fat compared to bones and muscle tissue, and the way that this fat is distributed.

The Physics of Swimming

On the whole, swimmers pull diagonally rather than straight back due to water resistance. If a stroke were purely efficient, it would be possible for the swimmer to pull straight back. Newton's third law of motion means that if you push water backwards, an equal force will be produced in the opposite direction, i.e. in pushing your body forwards. The result has been a compromise between man and water and man has learnt to pull diagonally quite effectively.

The other principal scientific theory that plays some part in swimming is Bernoulli's theorem. Often used as a basis for explaining the notion of lift in flight, when applied to swimming, it means that when the hand travels through water, the water over the upper side of the hand travels faster than the water moving under the palm of the hand. The resulting effect is that there is a difference in pressure on the two sides of the hand, which creates a lift force. When this lift force is confronted by the drag force on the hand, it produces a resultant force that drives the body forward.

The point where the hands begin to purchase the water is known as 'the catch'.

The Catch

The rotation of the hands and forearms during swimming helps to create purchase on the water. In all the strokes, there is a point during the pull where the hands stop paddling and begin to purchase. This is known as the catch.

The Four Sweeps

The four strokes consist of a series of circular movements known as the four sweeps: the outsweep, downsweep, insweep and upsweep. These sweeps consist of sculling movements and can be found at different points in the arm strokes for all four strokes. While freestyle and butterfly start with a downsweep at the beginning of the arm-pull, the breaststroke and butterfly pull start with an outsweep in a curvilinear movement. The way each swimmer handles each of these movements determines the effectiveness of the stroke.

Balance and stability

Balance and stability in swimming are the ability to maintain a streamlined position. Better streamlining means more efficient movement in the water, which in turn means faster times when racing.

Building Core Stability

A well-used phrase among swimming coaches and physiotherapists is 'core stability' – the ability to control the position of the trunk and lumbar spine during dynamic movement. Good core stability makes for a more streamlined position in the water and more efficient use of the arms and legs. It's where your main power comes from. It holds the trunk in good alignment to prevent snaking down the pool (which is clearly a wasteful use of energy), rotational problems in the stroke and a drop-off in leg power over the last 10 metres of a race. It is also thought to help prevent injuries. Poor core stability, on the other hand, means you can't hold your body position in the water and will have reduced power from the limbs.

'Because your arms and legs are attached to that middle section of the body, greater strength and control of the middle section means you have more strength in your arms and legs, and your propulsion through the water is better,' says Diane Elliot, physiotherapy and sports science co-ordinator for ASA England Talent. 'If you have poor core control or core stability, your pelvis will tend to drop, adding drag in the water.'

Core stability is not pure strength, but a combination of strength and control of the

Good core stability makes for a more streamlined position in the water.

trunk. Some people naturally have better core stability than others, but it can be improved through a programme of exercises, such as Pilates and posture work.

Improving Your Streamlining

Elliot offers the following advice on streamlining: 'It's an awareness of your body position in the water. A lot of it is to do with posture. If you have poor posture it makes it much harder to recruit

Good streamlining also helps buoyancy, although some people are naturally more buoyant than others due to the shape of their body, lung volume or fat content. Women have more fat than men so are more buoyant. People whose pelvis is tilted forward may be able to run faster, but are likely to be less buoyant because the naturally arched back makes it harder to adopt a flat body position in the water.

the right muscles. Poor posture is typical of swimmers. You see many with round shoulders. Then, in trying to achieve a more streamlined position, they tend to arch their backs and become more curved. Arching means your abdominal muscles are longer so you can't recruit as well.'

Efficient swimming and resistance

F1 teams invest millions of pounds to save fractions of a second by reducing drag as their cars carve through the air. Despite the obvious differences, the principle is shared by swimming. Improved body shape, technique and streamlining will all cut down resistance and lead to faster swimming.

Too much muscle tissue can be problematic because it increases form drag, which is caused by the body being insufficiently horizontal. Similarly, too much fat can also increase this type of drag. The ideal body shape for swimming is often considered to be wide shoulders, thin tapering hips, long arms and legs and big feet and hands, all allied to a lean physique. Although there have been successful swimmers who do not have these attributes.

Form Drag

Speed causes drag. You need to bear in mind that when you double your speed, probably when you are racing, the amount of drag increases by a factor of eight. If one were to view a swimmer

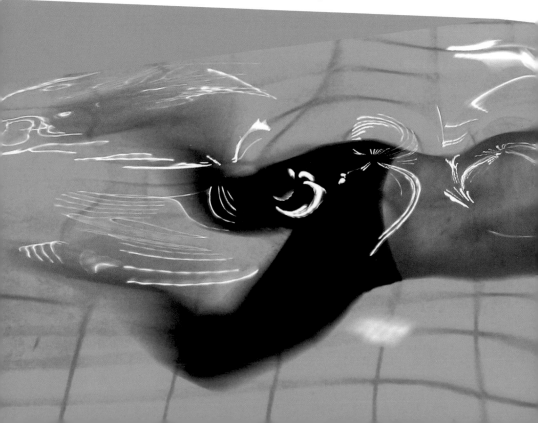

travelling through water from the side, the less horizontal that swimmer, the greater the form drag. Form drag can be reduced by keeping the hips and feet as close to the surface as possible, but also occurs laterally when the head is turned too far to the side. This twists the hips out of line and skews the body to the side.

Wave Drag

This form of drag occurs around the water surface and is increased by the swimmer causing too big a wave when the limbs or torso break the surface of the water. The overall effect is to create a water barrier in front of the head. This form of turbulence can act as a brake on forward movement.

Frictional Drag

The introduction of skin-tight swimming suits in recent years has come in response to a demand for the reduction of form and frictional drag. Frictional drag is about the effect of a swimmer's body on water molecules. Smooth or still water creates less friction with the body, but laminar- or streamline-flow can be interrupted by frictional drag. This type of flow occurs when water flows in parallel layers.

Reducing drag leads to faster swimming.

Breathing

For the novice swimmer, breathing is often one of the hardest challenges that they need to master – but it's important for the more advanced swimmer too. Correct breathing techniques vary from one stroke to another, but in each case efficient breathing is integral to better swimming.

At all stages on the swimmer's pathway, breathing plays an important part. Unlike other stroke mechanics, faults are difficult to identify and often difficult to see. The main considerations for efficient breathing are regularity of inhalation and exhalation, avoiding straining the neck muscles, keeping the head close to the water surface and expelling carbon dioxide on a regular basis.

Basic Principles

You will need to develop a comfortable breathing pattern that meets your needs. The first challenge is to balance the pressure of the air inside the nose with that of the water outside, in order to prevent water rushing up your nose when your face is in the water. One way of overcoming this problem is to practise blowing air out in the instant before your nose goes into the water. This helps to create an air pocket when your face goes underwater.

Breathing for Freestyle

If we take freestyle for example, some swimmers prefer to breathe to one side only, while others find it better to use alternative or bilateral breathing. The advantage of the latter form of breathing is that it helps to reduce lateral movement by breathing every three strokes, and maintains propulsion. It also helps to facilitate balance and equal power in both arms. A further form of breathing is to take four strokes. This can be tiring and is generally only used for sprint races. Breathing every four strokes is a useful hypoxic (working without air) training exercise, particularly if used for arms-only training, where it can be used to develop the cardiovascular system.

In general, it is better to avoid building up too much fatigue, even in 100m races, by avoiding keeping your face in the water for too long. In short sprint

Frontcrawlers should try to keep their nose at water level as they breathe in.

races, oxygen deprivation is less of a factor and, after a period of training, better swimmers can swim 50m races on butterfly and freestyle on one or two breaths. When first mastering freestyle a common mistake is in rotating the head too far back towards the shoulder. Try to keep your nose on the water as you breathe in. Lifting the head is a similar and often connected problem, which can be easily diagnosed. When swimming freestyle, try to avoid the breathing interrupting your natural body roll.

Butterfly and Breaststroke

In butterfly, most swimmers take a breath on every stroke or every other stroke. Breathing every three strokes would, for average competitive swimmers, be just too tiring. Two breaths-one breath breathing patterns do, however, work well and are less exhausting. Breaststroke breathing should occur once in every stroke cycle and forms part of a wave effect in which the head is lifted to take a breath and then thrust forward as the arms are straightened in front of the head. The air is then expelled in two strong breaths through the mouth. Among the early errors that swimmers make is to lift the head too high in butterfly and breaststroke, thereby spoiling the horizontal body alignment.

Breathing for Backstroke

In backstroke, it is often the case that swimmers do not breathe out fully. Regular breathing patterns, such as breathing out on one arm and in on another, should be accompanied by exploding the breath into mid-air to ensure that as much carbon dioxide as possible has left the lungs.

Butterfly swimmers should avoid the temptation to lift the head too high when breathing in.

Breaststroke breathing occurs once in every stroke cycle to form part of a wave effect.

The strokes

There are four main racing strokes in swimming: freestyle – which normally takes the form of frontcrawl – backstroke, breaststroke and butterfly. Swimming strokes have followed an evolutionary pattern, undergoing a number of rapid changes in the mid-1800s, and developing into the strokes we see today.

Frontcrawl

A freestyle race means just that – you are free to use any stroke that you wish. In practice, however, frontcrawl is the fastest stroke and is therefore the choice of every competitor in elite freestyle events and the vast majority at lower levels.

Freestyle – or frontcrawl – is the fastest of the strokes and is therefore considered to be the most efficient. As soon as you become proficient, you can get up considerable speed using the stroke. In 1976, man broke the 5 miles an hour speed barrier for the first time, and we have gone on getting faster ever since.

We have probably all tried dog paddle but its senior partner, frontcrawl, is more complicated. The strange fact is that while it is the fastest stroke, there is

no specific frontcrawl event in the racing programme. Frontcrawl is normally employed in freestyle races. Freestyle races are so called because the swimmer can choose whatever stroke he likes. The reality is that nearly everyone employs frontcrawl.

Keep It Smooth

How then can you master frontcrawl? The answer is normally in the streamlining. Good frontcrawl is a series of continuously propulsive inter-connected movements. Any unnecessary movement to the side will result in an opposite movement, and this movement results in the body snaking its way down the pool. The swimmer tries to make all the stroke

transitions – whether it is to breathe, propel, or paddle with the arms – as smooth and well connected as possible. The best analogy we can think of is that of swimming down a narrow tube with a diameter of about one metre. The idea would be to make all your movements without touching the sides of the tube.

On a Roll

There also needs to be a certain amount of body roll so that the breathing can be made to the side. In order to avoid too much roll, when turning the head to breathe, keep the nose on the surface. The air should then be taken in through the mouth and blown out through the mouth, although the effect of this is for carbon dioxide to be expelled through mouth and nose.

In Sequence

Most people breathe to the right, so the sequence for frontcrawl involves turning the head to the right as the left hand enters the water. Once the swimmer has breathed in, the head is brought to the front with the eyes focused on the bottom of the pool about a metre in front. At this point, the hairline needs to be kept on the surface of the water. The right arm now enters the water with the fingertips leading the movement. For people who find it more comfortable to breathe to the left, the sequence will be the other way round.

In frontcrawl, the head turns to the right as the left arm enters the water – or vice-versa for left breathing.

Frontcrawl explained

Frontcrawl is the only competitive stroke swum on the front which requires alternate limb movements rather than symmetrical actions. Swum well, it looks and is fast and efficient.

Right-arm Action

The arms move in an alternating and opposite pattern. In the case of someone breathing to the right, when the right arm enters the water, the hand slides forward just under the surface and the arm is extended in a line by straightening the elbow. This arm is then pulled back to the right-hand hip by bending the elbow and pressing back with the hand under the stomach and then down to the stomach and thigh. Water pressure forces the arm to take an 's'-shaped path.

Left-arm Action

During this phase, the left hand has also been on the move, taking up the opposite position. As the right arm enters the water, the left arm pulls through at the left hip. At this point, the elbow bends and the lower arm hangs down with the left hand and fingers pointing towards the surface in a relaxed manner. The left arm extends forward to enter the water in front of the head, on the body's centre line. This is an imaginary line down the centre of the body as it lies on the surface of the water. The aim is to slide the hand so that it is fully extended in front of the head.

Controlling Your Elbows

Throughout the arm cycle, the elbows need to be bent and held perpendicularly during the recovery of the arm. The best way to achieve this is to show more and more of the armpit as the arm is recovered. During the pull, the hand should always accelerate towards the stomach and thigh. At the end of the pull, the hand sculls outward under the trunk so as to be wide of the shoulder line. There are therefore two sweeping motions: one that is down and inward under the body when the arms pull towards the stomach, and the other at the end of the pull as the hand goes out and upwards past the hips prior to being recovered over the water.

Avoiding Common Errors

There are several errors that people make when learning frontcrawl – avoiding them can make the stroke less tiring. Training the legs to kick effectively is a forerunner of good crawl. Always keep the legs under the surface of the water. The heels should just break the surface. The leg action emanates from the hips. Try to keep the legs as straight as possible when kicking down.

Although you should aim to point down towards the bottom of the pool, the natural roll of the body means that the legs are never at 180 degrees to the bottom of the pool. Try to keep your feet moving rhythmically and get your arm action into a rhythm with which you feel most comfortable.

As the right arm enters the water, the left arm pulls through at the left hip.

As the right arm reaches the point of maximum extension, the left arm is beginning the recovery phase.

Water pressure forces the pulling arm to take an 's'-shaped path.

During the pull the hand should always accelerate towards the stomach and thigh.

At the end of the pull the hand sculls outward towards the trunk so as to be wide of the shoulder line.

Throughout the stroke cycle, the elbow needs to be bent and held perpendicularly during the arm's recovery.

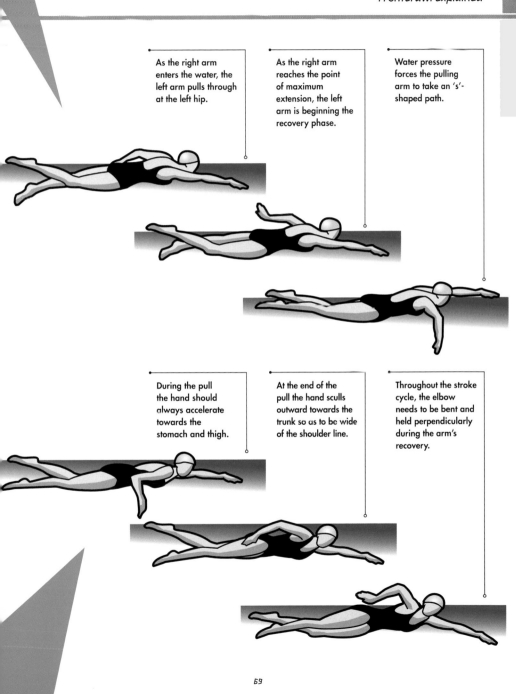

Frontcrawl specialist tips

The power of frontcrawl comes mostly from the underwater pull – but its effectiveness can be improved or reduced by a range of other factors. The rhythm of the kick, breathing technique, a good arm recovery position and a well-balanced stroke all contribute to an overall efficiency.

In general, your frontcrawl arm movement needs to fit in with the rhythm of your legs. Everyone has their own way of timing the frontcrawl, for example based on your body type and the level of efficiency achieved with your breathing. A number of different leg kicks can be applied to each arm cycle (a complete movement of both arms through 360 degrees). Many people make six leg kicks to each complete arm cycle. This normally comes about when the stroke is quite long with the arms extended

well out in front, and the hands pushed through right past the hips. Generally, this kick is employed when you are swimming at speed.

Swimming at Distance

When swimming at distance, many people find a six-beat kick too tiring, so often employ a four- or two- beat kick with a cross over. A cross-over kick is normally used by swimmers who need to turn their heads to breathe in a more pronounced manner. Here, the legs move laterally

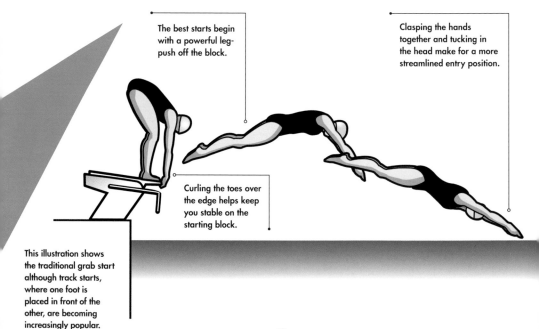

The best starts begin with a powerful leg-push off the block.

Clasping the hands together and tucking in the head make for a more streamlined entry position.

Curling the toes over the edge helps keep you stable on the starting block.

This illustration shows the traditional grab start although track starts, where one foot is placed in front of the other, are becoming increasingly popular.

to the side in order to provide balance for the stroke, but do not complete a downward movement. If you are seeking to swim to keep fit, two or four kicks for each leg cycle should do the job.

If you find that your legs tire quickly, it may be as much to do with your breathing as your technique. Put simply, if you do not fully exhale under the water, you may find you get a build-up of carbon dioxide. Ensure that you have used up all the air you inhaled on each arm cycle before completing that cycle.

Pulling Through

Great swimmers paddle more effectively to the next propulsive phase in their arm strokes than most other people. The pull under the water is therefore of great importance, but the recovery over the water is equally important. Frontcrawl is comprised of a range of angular movements. For instance, the elbows should be bent to 90 degrees with the fingers pointing towards the water during the recovery phase. The hand enters slightly cupped at a 45-degree angle, then extends just under the surface of the water until fully extended in front, before starting the pull. While this is taking place with one arm, the other arm needs to pull right back past the hips before being recovered.

When you begin the pull, try not to let your elbows drop. This is best achieved by attempting to pull with the lower part of the inside of the forearm, as well as the hand. If your hands recover too high over the water, aim to lightly scrape your fingernails along the surface as your hands move to the front. This reminds you to keep your elbows nice and high.

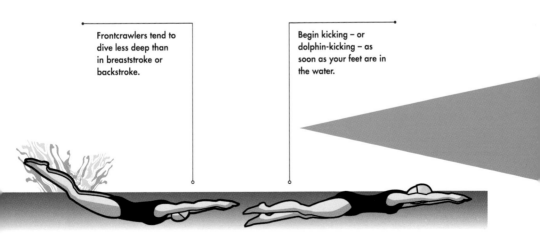

Frontcrawlers tend to dive less deep than in breaststroke or backstroke.

Begin kicking – or dolphin-kicking – as soon as your feet are in the water.

Frontcrawl turns

There is no rule that says you have to tumble-turn but an efficient tumble unquestionably produces faster times. Somersaulting or 'tumbling' into the wall and touching only with the feet rather than hand and feet enables the freestyler to complete the turn with minimal interruption to the motion.

The Tumble Turn

It will take time to perfect the tumble or flip turn, which is the turn primarily used for frontcrawl. The tumble turn is a very quick and compact way of making use of the wall. A good strong push off with the body in an optimum position about a foot under the water can pay rich dividends. A strong push off and glide is quicker than simply swimming away from the pool wall. Streamlining remains all-important, with good swimmers seeking to balance the body with the eyes facing down to the bottom of the pool, and the body stretched out in one straight line before taking the first stroke.

Practising in the Pool

The best way to start to learn is by concentrating on the 360-degree rotation of the body. This can be achieved by first making a somersault in the middle of the pool. Either stand in water sufficiently deep for you to be able to move through 360 degrees, or lie flat on your front in deep water. Now, tuck your knees up to your chest and your chin down to your chest. At the same time, pull towards your hips with your hands. The hands should be in line with the hips, fingers facing down. Keep tucked in and you will go through a complete circle. The aim should be to make the whole movement vertical.

Practising against the Pool Wall

When this has been mastered and you can rotate quite quickly, the next stage is to try the same movement against a pool wall. Attempt this at a slow pace, paddling with your feet towards the wall with your hands out in front of you. Take a deep breath and remember to drop your chin down to your chest to aid the rotational movement. As your feet rotate over your head, feel for the wall with your soles and then push off on your back. This means that the soles of your feet will meet the wall with your knees still bent. Your aim is to extend your body by drawing your hands up by your sides and stretching them above your head with the ears covered by the inside of your arms. Finish up with a backstroke glide.

If you are able to manage this movement, the next stage is to work on pushing off on your front. This is far from easy, mainly because you will be slightly disorientated from rotating through 360 degrees. To help with this, you need to keep in mind that, as soon as you feel your feet hit the wall, you need to turn your nose to face the bottom of the pool. The rest of the body will naturally follow your head and the plane it has adopted. At the same time draw your arms up, keeping your hands close to your body. Your hands are then placed close to your ears, and you

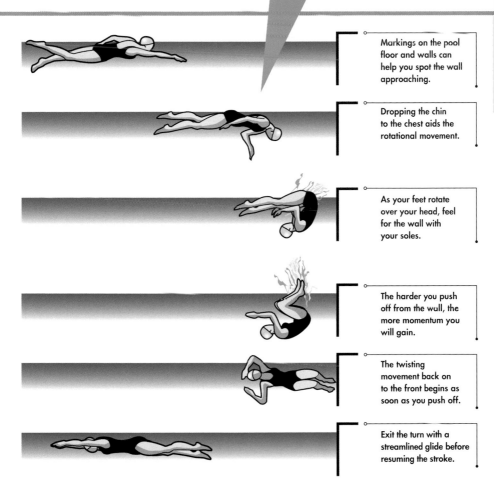

Markings on the pool floor and walls can help you spot the wall approaching.

Dropping the chin to the chest aids the rotational movement.

As your feet rotate over your head, feel for the wall with your soles.

The harder you push off from the wall, the more momentum you will gain.

The twisting movement back on to the front begins as soon as you push off.

Exit the turn with a streamlined glide before resuming the stroke.

extend the arms as your body stretches into a glide. During the whole of this movement, your hips will have dropped slightly at the wall. It then becomes a matter of trial and error until you can bring your body to the most streamlined push-off position.

When streamlining from the wall on the push off, practise until you can take between four and eight strong but shallow vertical dolphin kicks. Usually these kicks start deep and get shallower.

This will aid your get away from the wall and allow you to travel up to 10m away from the wall whilst streamlining.

Standards to Aspire to
100m Frontcrawl

	Senior	U17	U15	U13
Men	0:53	0:54	0:56	0:59
Women	0:59	1:00	1:04	1:02

Standards taken from qualifying times for 2011 senior, youth and age group national championships.

Backstroke

Backstroke has evolved almost beyond recognition since its early days, when it was really breaststroke upside down. 'Old English backstroke' is still legal, and still used by some older master swimmers. But modern backstroke – backcrawl – is undoubtedly faster and more efficient.

Backstroke Beginnings

Backstroke started life as a form of inverted breaststroke. Swimmers used to race with both arms pulling and recovering together, with a breaststroke kick. The stroke began to be swum with the arms similar to today's action, with one arm alternating with the other, then in the 1900s people started to realise that it was more efficient to flutter the legs in a frontcrawl style. Backstroke is particularly useful to those who prefer not to swim with their face in the water. It is similar to frontcrawl, except that the face is always clear of the water so that turning the head to breathe is not required.

Head Position

In backstroke, the head should be kept as still as possible with the spine and head in one line. The arms and legs move around this fixed central position. The head rests lightly on the surface of the water with the eyes fixed in one position. Normally this fixed position is based on individual comfort, but it also needs to take into account body streamlining so that the head does not cause too much resistance. This means that the eyes should be set at about 45 degrees from the vertical with the chin tucked in slightly towards the neck. Very little water should break over the forehead as the body arrows through the water. As a guide, the surface of the water should be just beneath the level of the chin, and just over the ears.

Some backstrokers test their ability to keep their head steady by balancing a cup of water on their foreheads while they swim. One way of finding out whether you have adopted a good position is by asking a friend to observe whether water is coming over your forehead.

Hips and Hands

Your hips should be close to the surface and the leg-kick made with nearly all the action under the surface of the water. You may not be used to swimming on your back and it is therefore a good idea to identify a landmark on the side of the pool or on the roof that indicates when you are getting near to the end of your length. It is also a good idea to first try backstroke when the pool is a little quieter.

Swimming backstroke feels a little like rowing a boat in that the hands, which act like paddles, begin to pull from a position where they are fully outstretched on the water surface in front of the head. From this position, the hands then pull until they reach a fixed position in the water almost in line with the shoulders. Having reached this fixed position, they push the body past it. This scenario takes place on each arm stroke.

Breathing Pattern

One of the early errors that people make is to forget to breathe out. You need to expel carbon dioxide continuously. Find a rhythm that suits you best but generally, the breathing pattern consists of breathing in on one arm-stroke and out on the other. The outward breath should be made explosively from the mouth.

Backstrokers start by throwing themselves away from the wall with arched backs.

Backstroke explained

Like frontcrawl, the complete stroke is almost continuously propulsive. The arms follow a rowing-like motion, with most of the movement kept outside of the body line.

Backstroke movements are less powerful than in frontcrawl, where you are able to pull under your body. The arms alternate and are swept backwards. If you imagine the body as a clock, the arms enter the water between 1 and 2 o'clock and between 10 and 11 o'clock. On entering the water, your arms should be kept straight and hands turned with the palms facing outwards. The arms are driven back deep behind the head into the water to increase the range of their pull. This is further facilitated by a shoulder roll, which takes place while your head stays still, as does the central vertical axis of the whole body. Your hands can either be turned out or face down towards the surface as they are recovered over the water; generally they are turned out to prepare for hand entry.

Hand Position

As your left hand enters the water, your right hand has completed the pull phase of its cycle, and vice-versa. Your hands will be approximately at opposite points in the arm cycle to one another. The little finger enters the water first and is then driven down to approximately 40 centimetres below the surface. At this point your arm should be kept relatively straight. The idea is to get the hand to a position where it can pull on still water that is relatively undisturbed. You should now cup the hand slightly and begin to pull back towards your feet.

Pulling Through

The pull towards the feet is a long movement, and the pressure of the water forces the arm through a three-phase motion in a downwards-upwards-downwards pattern. Almost unknowingly you will adjust your hand position to deal with this resistance. The initial movement is with a straight arm but immediately on entry the arm starts to bend at the elbow, and by the time it has reached a position where it is in line with the shoulder, the elbow is bent at 90 degrees. The hand is now sideways to the shoulder and in line with the forearm. At this point, water resistance has forced the hand upwards. The final propulsive phase now consists of your forearm extending and your hand pressing downwards to the hips. By this time, your hand will rotate at the wrist so that it passes slightly beneath the hips and finishes facing downwards. This movement, which is curvilinear, is counterbalanced by the other arm being recovered over the water. The recovery arm accelerates as it moves towards its entry into the water.

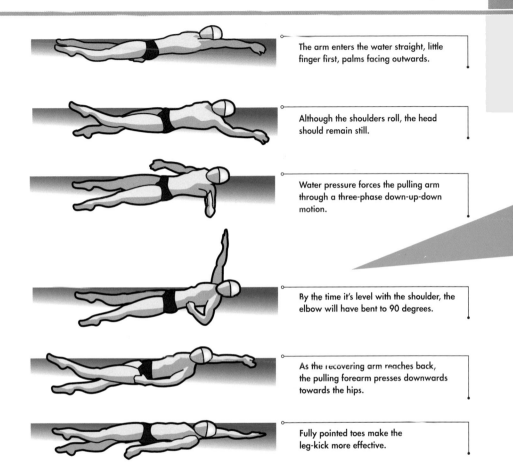

The arm enters the water straight, little finger first, palms facing outwards.

Although the shoulders roll, the head should remain still.

Water pressure forces the pulling arm through a three-phase down-up-down motion.

By the time it's level with the shoulder, the elbow will have bent to 90 degrees.

As the recovering arm reaches back, the pulling forearm presses downwards towards the hips.

Fully pointed toes make the leg-kick more effective.

Leg-kick

A good backstroke is normally accompanied by a strong leg-kick. The legs both balance and propel. There are a number of rhythms that you can adopt. The legs can kick at the rate of six, four or two beats, or two beats with a cross-over movement during each arm cycle. If you are swimming at speed, a flutter kick that utilises six beats will probably work best. In a similar way to frontcrawl, swimming backstroke over a distance may call for you to reserve more energy, so a slower leg action is more appropriate.

The knees bend slightly on the downward kick so that the feet hang down diagonally from the knees. Although you should kick up strongly, the toes should only just break the surface on the up kick. Try to keep your knees under the surface and the legs straight during the upward movement.

Backstroke specialist tips

Swimming on your back can be slightly disorientating, which in turn makes it harder to avoid simple mistakes. For those just getting to grips with backstroke swimming, here are a few tips to help overcome these problems.

Learning Backstroke

The best way to begin to learn backstroke is in shallow water. Try floating on your back in the first instance. Stand in the water and lower your shoulders to the water surface. Then place your arms out by your sides along the surface. Look up and let the water take the weight of your head so that the surface covers your head up to your ears. Next, stretch your legs out and point your toes so that the water gently lifts your legs. Once you have developed confidence and have tried this several times, you can move to stretch your arms out in line with your shoulders and start to move your legs up and down. When you have mastered this, you are well on the way to learning backstroke.

Avoiding Problems

When you are sufficiently proficient to be able to swim the stroke, you may find that, as you recover your arms, water runs into your face. If this is the case, try positioning your little finger and palm turned slightly outwards when lifting your arm out of the water.

Sometimes, early backstroke adopters find that the face goes under the water. This is normally a sign that there is too much roll in the body, and that a more fixed position needs to be adopted. Try to assume a more fixed position with your eyes. The best way to achieve this is by deciding on a point or a line on the pool roof, and fixing your eyes on it. If you find that you can hold your head steady but water still gets into your eyes and/or nose, you may need to tuck your chin in to your chest and look towards your feet.

If your leg-kick is quite weak, you might find that you tire quickly. You may also find that your legs are too low in the water, so you will need to adjust your eyes so that you are looking further behind your head at the pool roof. If you still continue to tire too easily, you may need to concentrate on breathing out much harder. Your arm movements can be made more powerful by lifting the shoulder prior to recovering the arm over the water.

Many swimmers swim straight by following a line on the ceiling. This is easier in some pools than others.

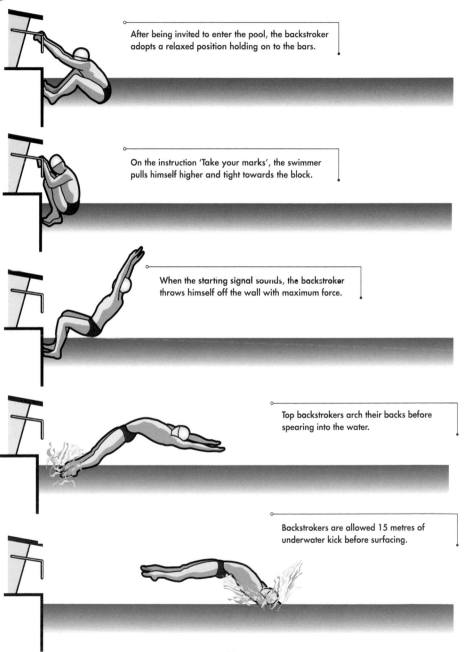

After being invited to enter the pool, the backstroker adopts a relaxed position holding on to the bars.

On the instruction 'Take your marks', the swimmer pulls himself higher and tight towards the block.

When the starting signal sounds, the backstroker throws himself off the wall with maximum force.

Top backstrokers arch their backs before spearing into the water.

Backstrokers are allowed 15 metres of underwater kick before surfacing.

Backstroke turns

A rule change in the late 1990s brought about significantly faster times as backstrokers learned to tumble-turn without touching the wall with their hand. It also led to some confusion among officials and swimmers alike – and to various technicalities that have to be observed.

Rules of the Turn

The backstroke turn is very similar to that of a freestyle flip turn. The rules require that, when executing the turn, some part of the swimmer's body must touch the wall. As part of the turning movement, the swimmer's shoulders can be 'turned over the vertical to the breast after which a continuous single-arm pull or a continuous double-arm pull may be used to initiate the turn. The swimmer must have returned to the position on the back upon leaving the wall' (FINA Rule SW 6.4). Formerly, swimmers had to remain on their backs throughout the turn, but the introduction of this rule meant that, during the turn, they could corkscrew on to their stomachs and back on to their backs. This means that swimmers can now apply a backstroke interpretation of the frontcrawl flip turn when racing.

There is one further law to be considered. A swimmer can carry out the whole turn entirely under the water, but must have broken the surface with their head after not more than 15 metres from the wall. This affords any swimmer the opportunity to carry out a series of dolphin leg-kicks during the glide phase prior to returning to the surface. A streamlined body position during the glide can aid this.

Practising in the Pool

As with the frontcrawl turn, it is best to start to develop the turn in the middle of the pool, concentrating on a 360-degree rotation of the body. This is closely described in the frontcrawl section (see page 72). When you have mastered all of the flip turn elements relating to freestyle, you are ready to reapply the sequence to backstroke. First, decide which way you prefer to roll. In this example, we'll look at leading with your right arm. Obviously, the movements will be reversed for turning around the left arm.

Start by lying on your back in the water about 5 metres from the poolside, then kick using backstroke legs with your arms down by your sides. About 1 metre from the wall, lift your right arm over the water and place it across the left-hand side of your chest, then seek the wall with the forearm of your right arm. As you carry out this movement, you should rotate through 180 degrees on your long body axis so that your head faces towards the bottom of the pool. You do not necessarily need to touch the wall but, in the early stages of learning the turn, it may help. Once you have adopted a position where your body is lying face down, you are now in a position to follow the sequence of the frontcrawl flip turn (see page 72).

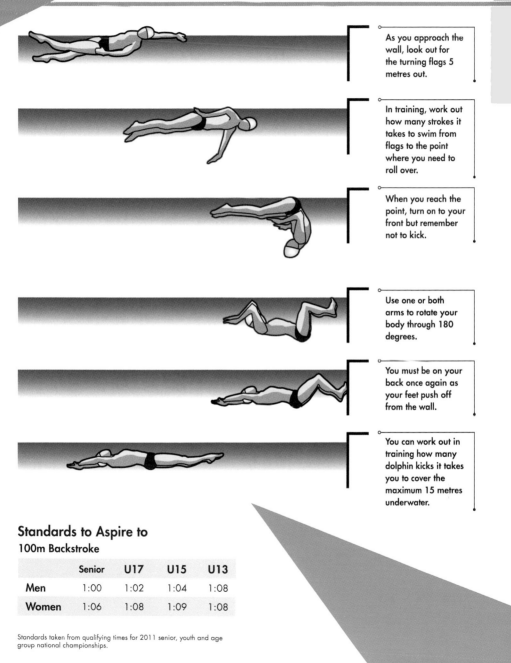

As you approach the wall, look out for the turning flags 5 metres out.

In training, work out how many strokes it takes to swim from flags to the point where you need to roll over.

When you reach the point, turn on to your front but remember not to kick.

Use one or both arms to rotate your body through 180 degrees.

You must be on your back once again as your feet push off from the wall.

You can work out in training how many dolphin kicks it takes you to cover the maximum 15 metres underwater.

Standards to Aspire to
100m Backstroke

	Senior	U17	U15	U13
Men	1:00	1:02	1:04	1:08
Women	1:06	1:08	1:09	1:08

Standards taken from qualifying times for 2011 senior, youth and age group national championships.

Breaststroke

The mechanics of breaststroke make it the slowest of the four competition strokes but it is also favoured by many leisure swimmers. But there are some major differences between recreational breaststroke and the techniques used in racing.

Types of Breaststroke

For those who are less serious, breaststroke's greatest advantage is that, as an option, it can be swum without the face coming into contact with the water. This presents the opportunity for two different types of breaststroke – one for those who are swimming for pleasure, where the head is held clear from the surface, and a second that is more associated with fitness and speed, in which the head is pressed forward into and, in some cases, under the water. The second version requires the head to be placed in the water and, according to the rules, for the head to also break the surface once in each arm cycle. The following sections will provide tips that help you to swim the second of these two versions.

Biomechanics of Breaststroke

Breaststroke is quite different to the alternating movements of frontcrawl and backstroke. It consists of four main sweeping movements – one in which the hands scull out and down from the centre of the body followed by a down sweep of the hands and a second in which the hands sweep back fast just below the surface of the water. Although the timing of the stroke is essentially that of pull, breathe and kick, the modern stroke consists of a series of partly overlapping movements. From a point where the body is in a straight line, you make the four sweeping movements with the arms. Before the arms are recovered in a straight line directly in front of the face, the head is lifted to breathe in. At this point, the legs

Today's top breaststrokers thrust their hands forward in a prayer-like position for maximum streamlining.

are bent at the knee so that the heels are drawn up to the backside. The aim is to breathe out as the arms are projected forward while kicking backwards and round. In breaststroke, timing is vital. As the feet whip together at the end of the kick, the arms have already overlapped and started the initial phase of the pull. This overlapping is designed to retain momentum.

In order to propel yourself as continuously as possible, you should aim to adopt a straight-line position at least once in every arm cycle. This straightening should take place when the hands and arms are stretched in front of the face. At this point, the whole body is in one line, slightly under the water. Straightening out in this way helps to get the best of the leg-kick before you go into the next stroke.

When swimming breaststroke, you should avoid carrying the head too high above the water and moving the head from side to side. Conjure up an image in which you are parting the water with your hands in order for your head and the rest of the body to travel through the parted water.

Breaststroke explained

Breaststroke is the slowest of the four competitive strokes and the one that is farthest from continuous motion. It relies more on a strong leg-kick than the other strokes while maximum streamlining is also advantageous.

Arm Action

The arm action begins with the arms and hands extended in front of the face. The palms of the hands turn to face slightly outwards as the outsweep begins. The hands pull out and slightly downwards. The motion of sculling out and sculling in plays a much greater part in the pull than the slight downward pull which can be identified when watching someone swim breaststroke. During this phase, your arms should stay straight. Your elbows start to bend as the arms move to the widest point of the lateral sculling action. This will vary from person to person but a distance of half a metre wide of each respective shoulder line provides a guide. At this point, your hands are approximately 15 centimetres under the surface. Your hands now start to scull inwards and, as they do so, the bend of the elbow increases. The next movement almost mirrors clapping the hands together under the chin. This is achieved by bringing your hands rapidly together under the chin as your pull comes to an end. As a general rule, during the pull, the arms stay in front of the shoulders and the hands, in front of the face. Throughout the outsweep, the elbows are higher than the hands. The shoulders are lifted clear of the water and adopt a shrugging posture as the hands cup in front of the face.

Kicking In

Once your hands have come together in front of your face and your upper body has adopted a higher position so you can breathe in, thrust the hands forward in a straight line in front of the face. The kick takes place at this point and the body is submerged. The exhalation consists of two phases: one at the start of the recovery forward and the second as the arms straighten out. This is accompanied by a strong, downward follow-through from the shoulders and upper body.

Your arms pull before your legs start to kick in each arm cycle. Throughout the leg movement, your feet should not break the surface. The legs move simultaneously and symmetrically. Start with your legs straight at the beginning of each arm cycle, when the body is in a straight line. Then bend your knees, keep your thighs together and lift your heels towards your buttocks. At this point, your feet stay just under the water. The soles of your feet are dorsi-flexed and should now fan out to face backwards in preparation for the backward movement. The legs straighten and, at the same time, the feet move circuitously with the toes remaining curled. Your aim should be to rotate the feet through as close to 180 degrees as possible. The heels are brought together and right at the end of the kick, the toes also whip together.

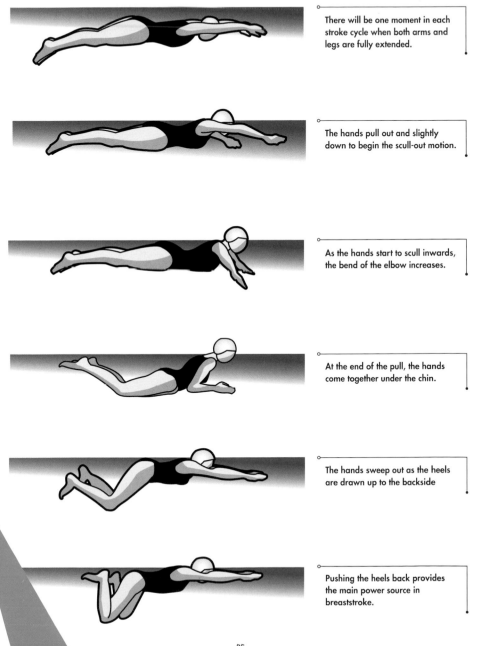

There will be one moment in each stroke cycle when both arms and legs are fully extended.

The hands pull out and slightly down to begin the scull-out motion.

As the hands start to scull inwards, the bend of the elbow increases.

At the end of the pull, the hands come together under the chin.

The hands sweep out as the heels are drawn up to the backside

Pushing the heels back provides the main power source in breaststroke.

Breaststroke specialist tips

Symmetry is the key word at every stage of breaststroke. The two arms and the two legs must move symmetrically, and any deviation – such as 'screw kicking' – will result in disqualification. Here are some tips to rectify such problems.

Avoiding the Screw Kick

The breaststroke leg movements are difficult to master, and the most common fault among those first getting to grips with the stroke is a screw kick. The expression 'screw kick' can cover a whole multitude of errors but the most common is a dropped knee, which means that the leg action is not symmetrical or that the toes on one foot bend back in a pointed manner. The main reason for this lack of symmetry is the pressure of the water on the curled toes and knee as the heel is lifted to the buttocks. This, in turn, makes the out-turned knee turn back under the body. If you are aware that you have a screw kick, one way of curing it is by practising breaststroke legs while up against the side of the pool. Try working on the leg action with your forearm and elbows resting against the pool wall.

If the problem still proves difficult to eradicate, try kicking breaststroke legs with your arms down by your sides. Reach with your hands to touch the soles of your feet before you kick back. This will help to reinforce the position of your

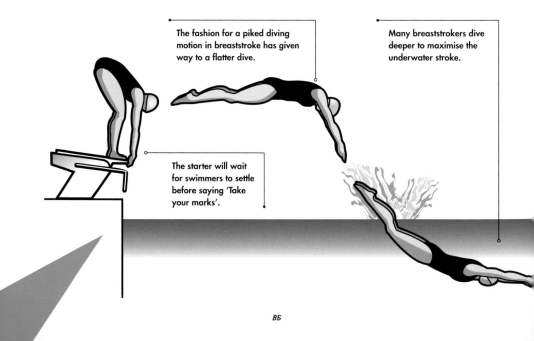

The fashion for a piked diving motion in breaststroke has given way to a flatter dive.

Many breaststrokers dive deeper to maximise the underwater stroke.

The starter will wait for swimmers to settle before saying 'Take your marks'.

legs before you kick. A further option is to turn your knees to each side to a greater extent than normal, and then to keep your heels together as they are drawn up to your buttocks. This will help you to feel where the legs are positioned and will avoid the build-up of water pressure during the movement of the heels towards the buttocks. You will then be able to turn your feet out and begin the whipping movement of the legs and feet.

There are some other considerations for the legs. Try not to draw the knees up under your body as they will act as a brake on the body's streamlining. In order to avoid this, concentrate hard on lifting the heels to your behind. If you have difficulty in kicking because your toes become too pointed, curl the toes as soon as you lift your heels to your behind.

Breathing Problems

During the early stages of mastering breaststroke, you may find that breathing correctly is an issue. For instance, you could find that water goes up your nose, particularly when you are recovering your arms. The best way to avoid this is by starting to breathe out before your face passes through the surface, thereby sealing off any inward rush of water into the nasal cavity.

Correcting Your Arm Action

There can also be difficulties with the arm action. One problem is in trying to control the in-sweep movement. You need to avoid pulling too wide, which makes it difficult to bring the hands back in front of the face. The trick is to avoid bringing the elbows too far back or, equally importantly, in bringing the elbows too far under the body during the pull. If you find that either of these faults occurs, start by reducing the heart-shaped movement of your arms to a very small circle, and slowly build back up until you can control the overall movement more easily.

For the underwater pull, breaststrokers may pull back their arms so they are tight to the sides of the body.

With the arms extended forward once again, the kick propels the body back to the surface.

Breaststroke specialist turns

Every breaststroker knows that you must touch the wall with both hands simultaneously at the turns and finish, yet a one-handed touch remains a common cause of disqualification. It's also faster to swim underwater but the rules allow only one stroke cycle under water after the start and each turn.

Elements of the Breaststroke Turn

In breaststroke, the race requirements for turns are that the touch should be made with both hands simultaneously at, above or below the level of the water line. One arm-stroke can be made after the push-off back as far as the legs, and a dolphin butterfly leg-kick is allowed during the first arm-stroke following a breaststroke kick. The breaststroke turn can therefore be considered to consist of the touch on the wall, the manoeuvre at the wall, the push and glide and underwater stroke following the glide.

Approaching the Turn

On your final stroke of the length, you should aim to approach the wall with your head down and your arms at long reach. The arms need to touch the wall together. As your fingertips touch the wall, your elbows start to bend and your torso starts to gather. Practice will determine whether you are more comfortable to turn to the left or to the right, but let us assume that you are making a turn to the left. Your legs should begin to bend at the knees before being drawn up. As this takes place, your left hand now withdraws from the wall. At this stage, your head stays down and your feet continue to be drawn up ready to push off from the wall.

In Transition

As you transfer your feet to the wall, your left hand stays in the water below the line of the body. This arm acts as a balancing agent while the right arm is thrown over the water. This right arm is normally bent and you should try to use a trajectory similar to a frontcrawl recovery movement. Effectively, the arm is thrown so that the right hand moves through a semi-circle over the surface. Your legs move under your body. Your right hand should now meet your left in front of the head and your body, which will have turned side on, pivots at the wall and rotates to the prone position. You are now ready to push off. The next stage is to plant the feet and squeeze the wall with the soles. At the same time, you need to straighten your elbows and arms.

Pushing Off

You should avoid having your feet too close to the surface. You need to allow your hips to drop slightly while turning at the wall. This will allow a deeper position for the push-off and glide. As the glide starts to slow under the water, you can now make a long pull down to your legs. Initially, this pull adopts the same form and plane as the breaststroke pull but, when the hands draw level with the shoulders, instead of sculling in

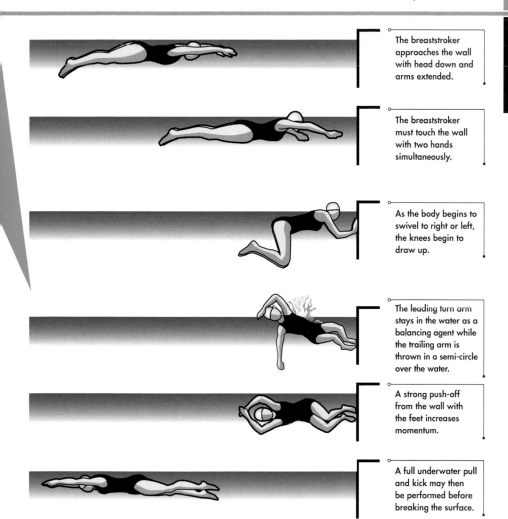

The breaststroker approaches the wall with head down and arms extended.

The breaststroker must touch the wall with two hands simultaneously.

As the body begins to swivel to right or left, the knees begin to draw up.

The leading turn arm stays in the water as a balancing agent while the trailing arm is thrown in a semi-circle over the water.

A strong push-off from the wall with the feet increases momentum.

A full underwater pull and kick may then be performed before breaking the surface.

front of the face, the hands continue to press back past the thighs towards the feet. When the arms are fully extended, they then start to recover to the front of the face in the same way as a normal breaststroke recovery. This movement is accompanied by a breaststroke kick, which will carry you back to the surface.

Standards to Aspire to
100m Breaststroke

	Senior	U17	U15	U13
Men	1:07	1:09	1:12	1:17
Women	1:15	1:18	1:18	1:20

Standards taken from qualifying times for 2011 senior, youth and age group national championships.

Butterfly

The newest of the four competitive strokes was born out of innovations by breaststrokers who discovered it was quicker to throw their arms forward above the water. It is widely regarded as the hardest of the four strokes but, when swum well, it is the most graceful.

Butterfly Evolution

Butterfly was first swum in breaststroke races but at the London 1948 Olympic Games, seven of the eight finalists in the 200m Breaststroke swam butterfly, leading to the view that butterfly and breaststroke should be seen as separate strokes with separate events. In 1952, it was decided to make the two strokes two separate races and these were held for the first time at the Melbourne 1956 Olympic Games.

Biomechanics of Butterfly

Butterfly is regarded as the hardest of the four strokes but, when swum well, it can be the most aesthetic to watch. One of the little-known facts about racing butterfly is that the legs and feet do not need to be at the same level when moving, but they do need to be simultaneous. Butterfly combines power and flexibility and, in order to reduce body drag, you should always try to keep your hips as close to the surface as possible. Approximately half a metre below the surface is the right height. The stroke consists of up and down movements in which the legs act as one and the arms swing forward together. The amount of vertical body movement or undulation should not be too great, as this can increase drag. It is therefore important not to lift the head too high to breathe, and to keep your chin no more than 8 centimetres above the surface. Try to get the water to carry the weight of your head as much as possible and avoid placing extra strain o n your neck muscles. When your head enters the water after taking a breath, fix your eyes on the bottom of the pool approximately 5 metres in front of a perpendicular position from your nose to the bottom of the pool. The arms enter the water in a swooping motion and the lower body mimics the movements of a dolphin in an up-and-down plane.

Butterfly is seen as the hardest stroke but also the most aesthetic when swum well.

Timing it Right

The timing of the movements is fundamental to success. One of the key dynamics is to lift the head out of the water before the arms come out, and to put the head back in the water before the arms go back in. This helps to avoid the unnecessa ry strain of carrying the weight of the head. These movements also accommodate the legs. Generally, most people swim with two leg-kicks in each arm cycle: one major downward kick and one minor.

The first leg-kick takes place as the arms enter the water and the head drops beneath the surface, and the second downward beat occurs as the hands push through at the end of the stroke. When you get to the stage where you can introduce the arms, you should kick down as you enter your hands and then apply a second kick as you press your hands back towards your feet. All the body movements consist of a series of rotations – at the hips and shoulders.

Butterfly explained

Rhythm and suppleness are crucial to good butterfly, helping to facilitate the dolphin-like undulation which in turn maximises the power of the arm-pull as the swimmer speeds through the water.

The arm stroke in butterfly is often described as an hourglass- or keyhole-shaped movement. This is due to the water pressing on the arms as they pull back from a position in front of the head to the thighs.

Arm Action

Your hands should enter the water just outside the shoulder line. The arms are extended in front of the head with the wrists cocked slightly so that the hands enter at about 45 degrees with the thumbs leading. The elbows are almost straight. Your first move should be to press the water down and back towards your stomach by applying pressure with the hands and forearms. The first part of the keyhole effect now in. You will find that water pressure forces your hands wide of your shoulders. When you first try the arm stroke, the pattern may be quite wide as you struggle to balance the movements but, with practice, you will find that it decreases.

At about half a metre under the water, the hands should start to catch hold of the water and grip more firmly. As a guide, try not to drop your elbows. Keep the elbows higher than the hands during the first part of the pull in order that you can fully leverage the water. As you catch hold of the water with your hands, you should then try to pull both hands towards your stomach. At this stage, the elbows tend to fix to facilitate the movement of the hands towards the stomach. When the hands have been pulled to a point where they are fractionally in front of and underneath your stomach, you should now push with your hands back towards your thighs with your middle fingers diagonally pointing to one another. If you were to take an underwater film at this point, you would see a large vortex around each hand, which dissipates but keeps the hands apart as you push back.

As the hands pass the stomach, the arms are almost at right angles at the elbow and your fingers should begin to face the bottom of the pool as you pull back with both arms to your upper legs. At the completion of the push, your hands should be pulled out of the water. At this point the palms face up towards the roof, and as you swing them forward together in a plane in line with the water surface, they slowly straighten after being bent at the elbows as they re-enter the water. During the recovery phase, the wrists rotate so that they start by facing up and slowly move to enter with the thumbs leading.

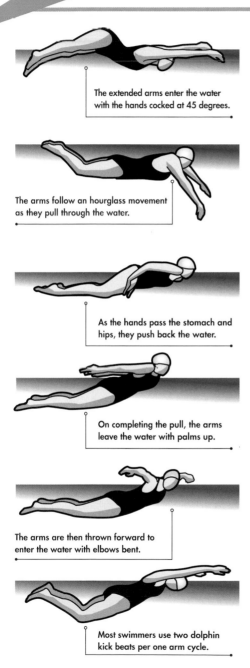

The extended arms enter the water with the hands cocked at 45 degrees.

The arms follow an hourglass movement as they pull through the water.

As the hands pass the stomach and hips, they push back the water.

On completing the pull, the arms leave the water with palms up.

The arms are then thrown forward to enter the water with elbows bent.

Most swimmers use two dolphin kick beats per one arm cycle.

Leg Movements

The leg movements are not too complicated. The key is to keep the legs together as much as possible. The feet should be loose so that the downward kick is made with the toes pointed. It should almost be like shaking your feet off. Your hips, knees and ankles should undulate. As the arms enter the water, they help to create an upward push of the hips. The first kick is partly a response to this and keeps the stroke flowing. It is something that will eventually come naturally without thinking too much about it.

During the two kicks, the knees should bend to about 120 degrees. The feet should relax in their recovery phase so that the weight of your feet is carried by the water. Your toes should be pointed on the downward movement, and remember to keep your heels under the water – about 4cm under is recommended. When the arms pull under water, the knees bend and the ankles relax during their recovery, ready for the second downward beat. This second kick drives the head up to take a breath.

Butterfly specialist tips

The key to quality butterfly swimming is in the kick. A common error among novice fly swimmers is to kick mostly from the knees. The real power comes from the hips, with the knees and feet playing a supporting role. Once this 'dolphin' technique is mastered, the difference is enormous.

Learning the Leg Movements

The best way to practise butterfly is to concentrate on the leg movements. Start by floating face-down in the water with your hands above your head, simply bouncing your stomach vertically up and down. Get the feeling of the hips, knees and feet working at a different point in the vertical plane. It should all feel quite easy and relaxed. Next, while keeping your feet together, try driving down towards the bottom. See if you can propel yourself forward. If you can manage this, stand with your back against the pool wall,

bring your feet up to the wall and allow your hips to drop down. Push off and try to make the same movements under the water. It should feel relaxing and, with practice, you should make headway.

Adding the Arm Action

You can practise kicking with a float later, but by far the most natural way is with your hands out in front. Once you are comfortable with the leg-kick, you can start to add the arm movements. Try this by taking a large breath, pushing off from the bottom in shallow water and

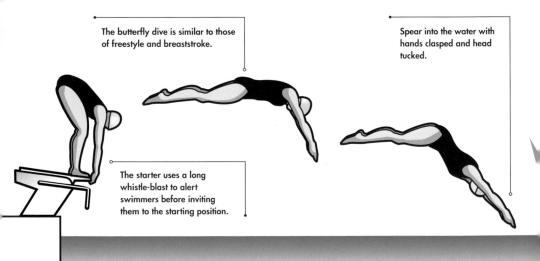

The butterfly dive is similar to those of freestyle and breaststroke.

Spear into the water with hands clasped and head tucked.

The starter uses a long whistle-blast to alert swimmers before inviting them to the starting position.

throwing your arms over the surface. Make one arm movement and then float forward, taking as many kicks as you need to stabilise yourself and keep your body moving forward. Slowly start to build this into two strokes, then three and more. Do not try too hard to work the kick in with the arms. Let the leg-kick fit in as naturally as possible. Once you have got the hang of it, you will be surprised how far you can go and how quickly you pick up butterfly.

Clearing Your Arms

Once you begin to improve, you will be faced by a number of common problems. One of these is getting your arms to clear the water on the recovery. If you experience this difficulty, one solution is to lower your head slightly when you place your head in the water by looking backwards towards your feet. You can then expel air strongly at the end of the arm-stroke and flip your fingertips high towards the roof at the end of the stroke.

You can also partly get round this by ensuring that the palms of your hands face out and rotating your hands at the last minute when they enter the water. If the palms of your hands face down during the recovery, your elbows will tend to catch the surface.

Kicking with Power

If you are getting insufficient power out of your kick, it is probably because you are trying to kick and pull at the same time. Always remember to kick at the start and end of the pull or, if you find this difficult, limit yourself to one kick in the early stages, either at the start or end. Finally, if you have difficulty with breathing and find that you swallow water at the end of the pull as your arms are starting to recover, it may be that you need to lift your head slightly higher and get your chin to clear the surface. To bring this about, you need to push back harder with your hands at the end of the pull, and make your down kick at the end of the pull phase much more positive.

The rules allow 15 metres of dolphin kick underwater.

Count your kicks in training to work out when you can safely surface before 15 metres.

95

Butterfly turns

The rules on butterfly turns have things in common with the other strokes. As in breaststroke, you must touch with both hands simultaneously at the turns and finish. And as in freestyle and backstroke, you can swim underwater for 15 metres before surfacing.

The butterfly turn has many similarities to its breaststroke counterpart. In competitive races, the rules are exactly the same as in breaststroke – swimmers are required to touch the wall simultaneously with both hands at, above or below the water surface. In addition, at the turn, swimmers are allowed one pull and any number of kicks under the water, which must bring them to the surface after 15 metres. If the head has not broken the surface after this distance, they are disqualified. Effectively, this means that after pushing off from the wall, the swimmer can swim underwater, but must keep the arms out in front of the head while making dolphin leg-kicks.

Approaching the Wall

When practising the butterfly turn, start about 7 metres from the wall and try to time your strokes so that you meet the wall with the arms extended at long reach. Your aim is to make the last stroke one long stroke. It is more economical to avoid making a further short stroke. As soon as your hands reach the wall, the elbows start to bend while your head continues to move to the wall along a horizontal plane. Your head should be just a few centimetres from the wall when you begin the actual turning movement.

Making the Turn

Choose which way you wish to turn by trying a turn in each direction and determining which feels most natural. At this point, the body concertinas and moves to a more vertical position. If we take a turn to the left as an example, your right arm remains on the wall while the main manoeuvre takes place. Next, your forearm moves to a position where it is parallel with the pool wall. The feet are now brought up under the body and your left arm provides balance by circling in the water with the palm facing down. Next you breathe in and your head should turn sideways. The feet are placed on the wall and your head now drops underwater. Your arms are drawn up above your head and you can push off with your hands effectively making a hole for your head through the water.

Pushing Off

With a little practice, you can quickly teach yourself how to make adjustments to get the best out of the push-off. Some Olympic swimmers kick underwater so effectively, particularly on freestyle, that their efforts are often called 'the fifth stroke'. With your body in the right position, you can travel at speed much further. You should aim to push deeper from the wall so that you can make first

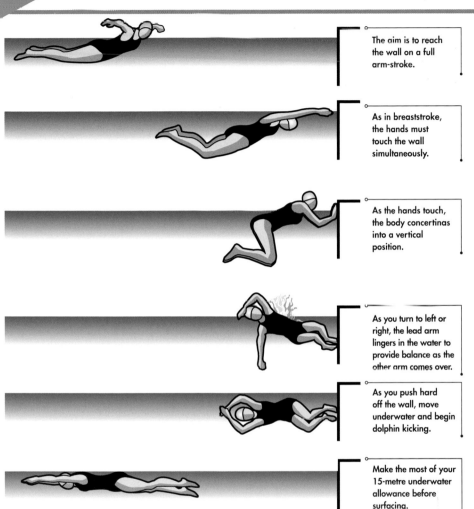

The aim is to reach the wall on a full arm-stroke.

As in breaststroke, the hands must touch the wall simultaneously.

As the hands touch, the body concertinas into a vertical position.

As you turn to left or right, the lead arm lingers in the water to provide balance as the other arm comes over.

As you push hard off the wall, move underwater and begin dolphin kicking.

Make the most of your 15-metre underwater allowance before surfacing.

one, then a number of kicks in their optimum position for propulsion. Try the push-off at a number of different depths. You are searching for deeper water that has been less disturbed by your body on your incoming length. This water should be more still and offer greater purchase for your movements.

Standards to Aspire to
100m Butterfly

	Senior	U17	U15	U13
Men	0:58	0:59	1:01	1:06
Women	1:05	1:07	1:07	1:09

Standards taken from qualifying times for 2011 senior, youth and age group national championships.

The events

Swimming events are built around the four strokes we have described – freestyle, backstroke, breaststroke and butterfly. The first Olympic Games in 1896 consisted of just four swimming events, contested in the sea. Gradually, more events have been added to the international and Olympic Games programmes.

Ω OMEGA

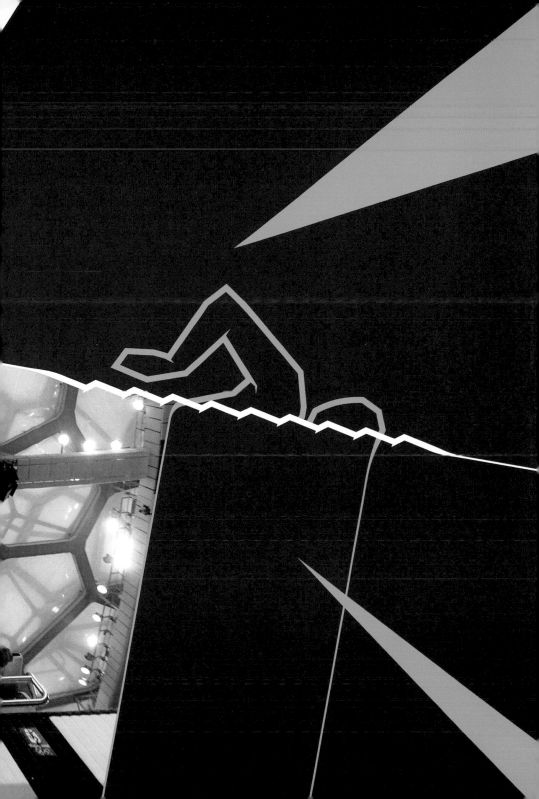

The 100m Freestyle is the blue ribbon event of Olympic swimming but the fastest man and woman in water are the winners of the 50m that was added to the programme in 1988.

The 50m and 100m Freestyle are swimming's most explosive events. They are both swum anaerobically – in other words, a swimmer taking part in these sprint events will increasingly draw from his lactic acid system. Fatigue sets in, which makes it harder to maintain speed through to the end.

How the Professionals Do It

Top freestylers concentrate on a strong six-beat leg-kick to each arm cycle. They get the maximum power out of each stroke by stretching well out in front on entering the arms, and pushing right through to the upper legs. The hand entry is normally soft, sliding rather than crashing through the surface. If you are going to take part in a sprint event, you will quickly observe that, in an effort to keep in a straight line, the better swimmers avoid turning their head too far or too often to breathe.

Rehearsal is the key to success. Olympic Games champion Alexander Popov maintained that he had rehearsed the events so many times that, when he competed, it felt like switching on the autopilot. There was clearly much more to his success than that. Like all top sprinters, he paced himself well. He would typically attempt to swim the second length of a 100 metres event only 1.5 to 2 seconds slower than the first. This is something you can only attempt with experience, and training time devoted to pace.

Alexander Popov

Alexander Popov started swimming at the age of 8 when his father took him for lessons. A backstroker for much of his life, he came under the guidance of coach, Guennadi Touretski, who switched him to freestyle with spectacular success. Popov achieved back-to-back wins in the 50m and 100m Freestyle at the Barcelona 1992 and Atlanta 1996 Olympic Games. Following the Atlanta Olympic Games, his career received a setback after he was attacked and stabbed in the street by a local vendor. Following surgery and a long period of rehabilitation, he returned to the sport, winning a silver medal in the 100m Freestyle event at the Sydney 2000 Olympic Games.

200m and 400m Freestyle

Sprinters regard the 200m as a tough event because it draws exclusively on the aerobic energy system. But that also makes this and the 400m Freestyle more tactical than the shorter distances.

How the Professionals Do It

Both of these events can generate great tactical battles. In the 400m, most top swimmers will try to negative-split the second half of the race. In other words, they will swim the first part at a steady pace, trying to reserve their energies for the second part of the event. In the 200m, it is a good idea to try to reserve energy. Swimming the second half of the race faster is an aspiration and the reality is that even the top swimmers complete the last 100m two or three seconds slower than the first, although part of the reason for this is the advantage gained in the dive.

Tactics play a great part, affecting the way in which you pace. In the 200m, the distance is too short to risk losing touch with the leaders by going out too slowly, so it is a good idea to make sure that during the first 100m you are at least on the shoulder of the leader. From this position, you are more capable of striking from the front. One of the greatest 400m tacticians was Australia's Murray Rose, who won the Melbourne 1956 and Rome 1960 Olympic titles. He often qualified for his finals in lanes other than those in the centre of the pool, catching opponents unaware by speeding up halfway through the race when most of his competitors were breathing on the opposite side and could not see him clearly.

Ian Thorpe

Australian Ian Thorpe, or 'The Thorpedo' as he was nicknamed, became arguably the most outstanding middle-distance swimmer of the modern era. Born in 1982 in Sydney, home of many other Australian freestyle greats, Thorpe's height of 1.95 metres (6ft 5in) and big hands and feet were great assets in his quest for medals. From 1998 to 2004, he dominated the 400m Freestyle event. In that time he won three gold medals at the Sydney 2000 Olympic Games in the 400m and two Freestyle Relays. He was disappointed to have finished with only the silver medal in the 200m but, at the Athens 2000 Olympic Games, he was able to make amends, winning both the 200m and 400m Freestyle gold medals.

800 and 1,500m Freestyle

Until the introduction of the 10km Marathon event at the Beijing 2008 Olympic Games, the women's 800m and the men's 1,500m Freestyle were the longest events in the Olympic Games programme. They remain the longest in the pool.

How the Professionals Do It

In 800m and 1,500m Freestyle, you should look for as even a pacing as possible. Only the first and last 100m are likely to vary. In the 2009 world championships, the Tunisian winner of the 1,500m, Oussama Mellouli, swam the first 50m in 27.42 seconds. Every length that followed between the first 50m and the 1,450m point was swum within a range of 28.95 and 29.95. Only over the last 50m did he speed up very slightly, yet the impression had been that he had been steadily getting faster from halfway through the event. The reality was that he was consistently registering laps that were within one second of one another. The best swimmers in the world, such as Rebecca Adlington, tend to dictate the pace from the start. They maintain an even pace throughout because they enjoy a superior level of fitness.

Race Tactics

In 800m and 1,500m races, swimmers seek either to pull away from or catch up with the nearest competitor to them in terms of race position. This gives each individual a target to aim for during the race. One tactic in distance swimming is for swimmers to swim on one side of their lane, away from an opponent. This has the double effect of making their competitor in the next lane, who may be looking underwater, feel they are further behind than they actually are. It also means that the swimmer in front is able to pull on undisturbed water.

Rebecca Adlington

Rebecca Adlington's win in the Beijing 2008 Olympic Games 400m Freestyle made her the first British woman to win an Olympic gold medal for nearly 50 years. Only a few days later, the Mansfield girl added the 800m title making her the first British swimmer to win more than one gold medal in swimming at a single Olympic Game since 1908. She finished six seconds ahead of silver medallist, Alessia Filippi, and her time broke Janet Evans's world record. The record had lasted since 1989. The significance of this performance was considerable as Rebecca was born in that same year, 1989.

100m and 200m Backstroke

As the only regulated stroke swum on the back, backstroke introduces unique skills to the competition programme, such as turning with the help of overhead flags and learning to swim in a straight line – which is especially hard in an outdoor pool.

Pre-race Preparations

When swimming backstroke, it is important to familiarise yourself with your surroundings. Backstroke racing outdoors can be difficult for those who have only experienced swimming indoors, where it is easier to determine where you are in the pool. Time spent in your pre-race warm-up or during practice sessions on turning and finishing will pay dividends in the race itself. Start at the backstroke flags and count the number of strokes to the wall. On the first attempt, try this at a medium pace. When you feel comfortable with this, try it at speed. In the case of both turning and finishing, when you race you will need to know exactly how many strokes are required. In the race itself, always finish with your arm straight and your hand well stretched out.

Starting Right

The backstroke start is also a key part of the race. Some swimmers pull themselves high on the wall. The rules permit you to lift your body as high as you want while holding on to the starting grips on the starting blocks. You start with your face looking towards the start end, with your body in the water. You are not allowed, however, to place your toes in or on the gutter. Goggles that provide protection from the glare of the sun are useful in outdoor racing.

Roland Matthes

Known as the Rolls Royce of backstroke swimming, Roland Matthes from Erfurt appeared to beat his competitors at will. His languid, long technique led to him completing each length in some 8 to 10 strokes fewer than some of his competitors. Born in 1950, he remained undefeated in international competition between 1967 and 1974. Matthes won the gold medals in the 100m and 200m Backstroke at both the Mexico 1968 and Munich 1972 Olympic Games as well as every other major gold medal in these events from 1970 to 1975 except for the 200m at the 1975 World Championships when he was eventually defeated.

100m and 200m Breaststroke

Britain's reputation as a nation of breaststrokers owes much to the victories of Anita Lonsbrough (Rome 1960), David Wilkie (Montreal 1976), Duncan Goodhew (Moscow 1980) and Adrian Moorhouse (Seoul 1988) – but it's almost 20 years since Britain won an Olympic Breaststroke medal.

How the Professionals Do It

Building your speed during a breaststroke race is, as with the other strokes, the cornerstone of success. When Adrian Moorhouse won the 100m Breaststroke for Team GB at the Seoul 1988 Olympic Games, his best and most vital stroke was his last stroke. Thrusting his arms forward with maximum power and taking the wall at long reach meant that he was able to pass the other finalists, just when it counted.

Starting Right

In breaststroke, as with the other strokes, the start offers you the opportunity to travel a distance at speed, while benefiting from the use of the pool deck to drive the body forward. Remember that you must adopt a start position in which at least one foot is placed at the front of the starting blocks and, if you start the race before the starting signal, you will be disqualified.

Training for Competition

Breaststroke is much more of a leg-dominated stroke than the other three strokes. The arms tend to play a larger part in the 100m event. Therefore, design your training to meet your event needs. This means, if you are planning for a 100m event, make sure you include plenty of arms-only training and, if you are swimming 200m, place more of an emphasis on legs-only training.

David Wilkie

Brought up in Sri Lanka, David Wilkie learnt to swim in the warm waters of Colombo Swimming Club. A reluctant trainer, Wilkie really started to progress when he was sent to board at Daniel Stewart's School in Edinburgh and he began training with Warrender Baths Club, one of Britain's top clubs at the time. By 1972, he had won the Olympic silver medal in the 200m Breaststroke in Munich and, just four years later, won the gold medal in Montreal, making him the only swimmer to have won Olympic, World, European and Commonwealth gold medals in the same event. Wilkie's world record-winning time was three seconds ahead of his nearest rival.

100m and 200m Butterfly

Good pacing is vital in butterfly swimming, especially over the longer distance. Swim too fast too soon and you'll regret it in the closing stages. Finishing on a full stroke rather than a half-stroke is also an advantage.

In a stroke as tiring as butterfly, controlling your pace is vital. Even the best swimmers can fade at the end of a race and, in 200m races, the second 100m can be swum as much as three or four seconds slower than the first.

How the Professionals Do It

At the Beijing 2008 Games, Michael Phelps (USA) never led the race until the last stroke, where the energy he had conserved in the first 50m meant that he was able to dramatically out-touch Miloslav Cavic (Serbia) by centimetres. Try, therefore, to race the first part of your event, particularly the 200m, with easy speed. This requires swimming as fast as possible with minimal effort, but will enable you to be stronger towards

the end. The trick is to train at your race distance so that you can carry out this form of controlled swimming faster than anyone else.

Race Tactics

During the first section of the race, keep your feet down and do not over-emphasise the kick. As you get towards the end of the race, in much the same way as racing on any of the strokes, gradually increase the range and power of your kick. A key factor is to train as close as possible to race-pace. If you swim at maximum speeds during training then it will help you, both at 100m and 200m, to become used to handling the latter part of the race whilst experiencing severe fatigue.

Michael Phelps

Six-times World Swimmer of the Year, Michael Phelps is widely regarded as the greatest swimmer in history and by some as the greatest Olympic athlete. He won six gold and two bronze medals aged 19 in Athens in 2004, and eight golds in Beijing four years later. His 2008 tally, which eclipsed the record seven golds achieved by fellow American Mark Spitz 36 years earlier, came in the 100m and 200m Butterfly, 200m Freestyle, 200m and 400m Individual Medley and the three Men's Relays, all but one in world record time.

200m and 400m Individual Medley

The individual medley – commonly known as the 'IM' – features all four competitive strokes swum in a specified order. It is swimming's greatest test of versatility and all-round ability.

The first individual medley champion was a British woman. Hilda James from Liverpool won the US National Championship in 1922 but it wasn't until 1953 that the first world record was inaugurated and the first Olympic competition wasn't held until 1964 when a 400 metres Individual Medley was introduced. Individual medley swimming is therefore not new but it was introduced to Olympic swimming programme later than the four strokes. Individual medley consists of butterfly, backstroke, breaststroke and freestyle.

It calls for strength and stamina, the ability to change from stroke to stroke at the turn and skills in all four of the main strokes. In short, it encapsulates all of the swimming skills in one race. Pacing is an important ingredient and, in the breaststroke leg, the slowest in time, you can make considerable headway compared to that of the other strokes. Many swimmers have different strengths and will apply different strategies to strokes that they are either weak or strong on, particularly if they know the strengths and weaknesses of the opposition they are competing against.

One way of working towards your first individual medley race, whether it is 200 or 400 metres, would be to take your best times for the 50 or 100 metres on the individual strokes. You can then add these together and then apportion a percentage to each of these times based on an ideal

Krisztina Egerszegi

Born in Budapest in 1974, Krisztina won her first gold medal when she was just 14 years of age. Known as 'Mighty Mouse', she overcame her lack of size with superior technical skill. Her world record of 2:06.62 for 200m Backstroke set in Athens in 1991 stood for a remarkable 17 years. Her major achievement was to be only the second female in Olympic history to win a gold medal in three successive Olympic Games, taking the 200m Backstroke title in 1988, 1992 and 1996. She added further gold medals in the 100m Backstroke and 400m Individual Medley in 1992.

time in which all four of your best efforts for the components are added together. You now have a framework with which to work. You can then set yourself a target time for either the 200 or 400 metres and work back with targets for each individual leg. If you know your race opposition, you may want to alter the weight given to one leg of the race.

Contemporary swimmers regard the 200 metres event as a sprint but will view the 400 metres very differently with effort often being made to balance the times on the first 100 metres on butterfly with that of the final 100 metres, the freestyle.

While the medley relay begins with a backstroke start, the IM starts with a dive for butterfly.

10km Marathon swimming

Until 2008, the longest event in Olympic swimming history was the 4-kilometre Freestyle, which was swum at the Paris 1900 Games. That all changed when Beijing 2008 hosted the first 10km Marathon swimming events, held in the Olympic rowing lake.

The Olympic Games Effect

Open-water swimming – competitions in the sea, lakes and occasionally rivers – has been around for generations in various forms. In fact the swimming events in the first four Olympic Games were all held in open water rather than swimming pools. But the addition to the Olympic programme of a 10km Marathon swim has changed the landscape dramatically. The lure of an Olympic medal has persuaded many distance pool-swimmers to double up or even switch events. Great Britain's David Davies, Keri-Anne Payne and Cassie Patten doubled up in Beijing with spectacular success, between them winning three of the six inaugural 10km Marathon medals, as well as competing in the pool events. Their success in turn has sparked a wave of interest in open-water swimming in Britain, with thousands taking part in the 'Great Swims' series that began in Windermere in 2008.

Mark Perry, Britain's open-water performance manager, believes open water is a natural extension to the repertoire of pool endurance swimmers, and not an alternative. 'If you've been a really good 800m or 1,500m freestyler, it's easier to move up to open water than down to 400m,' he says. 'Our swimmers don't train any differently to endurance pool swimmers. We have a firm belief that open water is about speed rather than just being able to swim for ever.'

Maarten van der Weijden

When 6ft-7in Maarten van der Weijden's sprint finish made him the first man to win an Olympic gold medal for 10km Marathon swimming, it also completed one of the most amazing comebacks in the history of sport. The flying Dutchman's 10km Marathon Beijing victory in 1hr 51min 51.6secs came five years after he won a two-year battle against leukaemia, which had threatened not only his swimming career but his life. The 27-year-old retired from swimming a few months later. 'He is the Lance Armstrong of swimming – it's inspiring,' said the silver medallist, Britain's David Davies, comparing van der Weijden to the American cyclist who won a legendary victory over testicular cancer.

Experiencing Open Water

The adage that there is no substitute for experience is especially relevant in open water. Fortunately there are now many opportunities to gain that experience over distances that range from a few hundred metres to the rather daunting 25km races held at world and European level. There are even one or two 40km lake swims in other parts of the world.

In Britain, while some hardy souls choose to swim outdoors all year round, competitive open-water swimming is naturally a seasonal sport. But such is its popularity that, if you are prepared to travel, it is now possible to compete somewhere in Britain on almost any weekend from mid-May to late September. The one-mile swims in the Great Swims series offer a good introduction to open water. Many events are held under the auspices of the British Long Distance Swimming Association (BLDSA) and are listed on their website (bldsa.org.uk). The Irish LDSA has a comprehensive programme (ildsa.info), while the ASA holds regional and national championships for various age groups (swimming.org).

Open-water swimming is riding a wave of popularity since Beijing 2008.

10km Marathon specialist tactics

The weather, the cold, waves, tides and currents, the tactics, food and drink, steamed-up goggles, no lane ropes, different costume rules and even seasickness – all these are among the factors that set open-water swimming apart from pool swimming.

Wetsuits and Swimsuits

In recent years wetsuits have become increasingly popular among triathletes anxious to keep out the cold and increase their buoyancy and speed. But wetsuits are not allowed under the rules of open-water or Olympic 10km Marathon swimming. Costumes must be made of the same textile fabric as those approved for the pool. Sleeves and zips are also banned, but under FINA rules open-water costumes can include full-length legs.

Hats

FINA rules allow up to two swimming hats, the BLDSA only one. In events where there is more than one category – such as men, women, different distances or age groups or separate breaststroke – organisers will often allocate a hat colour to distinguish the competitors in each category. Breaststrokers' hats must be white. Hats also reduce heat loss from the head.

Goggles

Goggles are widely used but can be troublesome because of the contrast between the warm body and cold water. This can cause them to steam up, but a quick splash of anti-fog spray or saliva on the inside of each eye-glass will do the trick. Some swimmers simply lick the inside of the eye-piece. Another trick is to allow a drop of water into each eye-piece before the start and then shake your head if they do steam up.

Water Conditions

FINA rules require a minimum water temperature of 16C for open-water events and stipulate that any current must

Acclimatising Your Body

Suddenly plunging from relatively warm air into cold water can come as a shock to the body, causing breathing problems and adversely affecting the opening moments of the swim. Britain's Cassie Patten, bronze medallist in the inaugural Olympic 10km Marathon swim in Beijing, recommends splashing yourself – especially your feet – before the race. 'I did my first race in South Africa. The air temperature was hot and when I got in the water the shock to my body was severe,' she says. 'My lungs closed and I felt I needed to breathe to keep going. If you get your feet cold, the blood from them will pump round and lower the blood temperature all around your body.'

be only minor. Beyond that, conditions can vary enormously, especially in the sea, where waves and changing tides can add to the problems facing swimmers. In choppy conditions, seasickness is not unknown. There is a popular misconception that long-distance swimmers grease up their bodies with a lubricant such as Vaseline to keep out the cold, but the main reason is to prevent chafing from their swimsuits.

Open-water Strokes
At national and international level, all events are freestyle. This means you can use any stroke or strokes, although frontcrawl is obviously the norm, being the fastest. Many BLDSA

Open water is a very tactical form of swimming.

events have a separate breaststroke category, however. Slower it certainly is, but breaststroke in this environment does have one small advantage over frontcrawl – breaststrokers generally swim straighter because they can see where they are going.

10km Marathon specialist tips

Talk to any seasoned open-water swimmer and they'll tell you that one of the biggest differences from pool swimming is the element of physical contact with other swimmers. In this arena, there are no lane ropes to separate you from your rivals!

Physical Contact

For many making the transition to open water, one of the first and biggest shocks is the physical side, which is absent from competitions in the pool. At times it can be more like water polo than speed swimming. According to the rules, 'taking advantage' of another swimmer by interfering or intentionally making contact with them is an infringement – as are pacing and slipstreaming. But with a mass start and no lane ropes, some contact is inevitable, especially at the turning buoys, where there may be a whole group of swimmers trying to take the shortest possible route around the corner, causing a funnelling effect.

Cautionary Cards

Sometimes it goes further with swimmers trying to gain advantage by pulling on the feet of the athlete in front or getting a tow by swimming too close behind. It's up to the officials to spot these infringements and take action. FINA rules specify a system not dissimilar to football, whereby the official raises a yellow flag and a card bearing the offending swimmer's race number for a first violation, and a red flag and card for a second offence. A red-flagged swimmer is disqualified and must leave the water and board an escort boat immediately.

The competitor's number is usually displayed in waterproof ink on the arms and upper back.

Swimmers wear numbers on their arms and upper back.

Eating and Drinking in the Water

As in the marathon run, marathon swimmers are allowed to receive food or drink during a swim. This can be dispensed either via a pole held out by the swimmer's coach from the escort boat, at a designated feeding station, or consumed from packs tucked into the costume. Individual squeeze gel packs containing a liquid mix of carbohydrates, antioxidants and amino acids, designed to provide an energy boost during the swim, are readily available in a range of shapes, sizes and flavours. Feeding need delay the swimmer for only a few seconds. You are allowed to tread water or even stand on the bottom as long as you do not walk or jump.

Open-water Tactics

Race tactics are another important aspect of open-water swimming. The most basic choice is whether to go out as quickly as possible or let someone else set the pace, making sure you don't lose touch. If the latter tactic is employed, you then have to decide at which point to hit the front. 'Tactics are the biggest learning curve,' says Mark Perry. 'Sometimes, swimming as fast as you can from beginning to end isn't enough to win the race. But being able to swim forever doesn't win races either. What wins is being quicker at the end of the race. Quite often, you get a race that isn't that quick and is just a sprint at the finish. But the world is still learning the ropes in this sport. I don't think anyone knows 100 per cent what they are doing.'

Olympic Games Relay events

Relay events occur at any time during the overall swimming meet and, internationally, when they come in the middle of the week, can place extra and quite different demands on swimmers to those of individual events.

Relay History
The idea of Freestyle Relay swimming has been part of Olympic competition since 1900 but the Medley Relay competition, which started life as just backstroke, breaststroke and freestyle, with butterfly later being inserted between the last two legs, appeared from 1953 onwards. The first Olympic Medley Relay events were held in 1960.

Freestyle Strategies
The most frequently used freestyle relay race-strategy is one in which the fastest athlete swims last, the second-fastest goes first and the remaining two take the middle legs. In swimming, there are other factors to be taken into account, such as the relative strengths of the teams in adjacent lanes and on which leg they are likely to place their swimmers; the water conditions and the level of wash from other teams; and the psychological impact of either leading or knowing that you have your best swimmers to come. Increasingly, team line-ups are meeting a wide range of parameters. Swimmers that have only three fast swimmers sometimes go for the fastest two swimmers first. There are no hard-and-fast rules.

Medley Strategies
There are no such considerations for the medley relay, where the running order is set out in the event rules and the only requirement is that each swimmer

Australian men's 4 x 100m Freestyle team

Before the Sydney 2000 Olympic Games, the USA had never failed to win the men's 4 x 100m Freestyle Relay – and anchor man Gary Hall Jnr predicted that they would 'smash' the home team 'like guitars'. But Australia's Michael Klim broke the individual world record on the opening leg and Chris Fydler and Ashley Callus kept the lead before Ian Thorpe held off Hall to win by 0.17secs in another world record time. Thorpe, just 18, leapt ecstatically from the pool to embrace his team-mates – and mock the defeated Hall by playing air guitar.

Takeover swimmers are allowed to move around while awaiting the arrival of their team-mate.

completes each leg using the correct strokes required for the corresponding individual event. In the medley, team managers are, however, often still confronted with decisions. For example, the best swimmer is quite often the fastest in two or more strokes, so judgements about the right combination and whom to place on which leg still have to be made.

The Takeover

One of the most contentious areas is in the relay takeover itself. The requirement in all relays is for one part of the outgoing swimmer to be in contact with the poolside when the incoming swimmer touches. This is more of a fine art than it first appears to be. Teams are disqualified for taking a flyer by going too early. This normally comes about either because the incoming swimmer takes an unexpected extra stroke or finds that he reaches for the wall but is unable to quite make it. Illness or injury to a swimmer can lead to last-minute team changes, resulting in teams that have not practised together. Sometimes, the outgoing swimmer fails to anticipate correctly and simply leaves too early.

Olympic Games Relay events explained

Relays are among the most consistently exciting races in the Olympic Games programme. Teamwork, team spirit and well-timed takeovers all come into play as rivals at national level pitch in for a common cause.

Two of the most notable relays in recent years have been the men's 4 x 100m Freestyle Relay finals at the last two Olympic Games. Both relays had something in common – to the uninitiated, the results were a surprise. But they differed in another way – one final underlined the value of good planning and teamwork, and the other, team spirit. All three are key ingredients in relay swimming.

Planning and Teamwork

In 2004, the USA arrived in Athens among the favourites to win the men's 4 x 100m Freestyle while South Africa were relative outsiders. The South Africans decided to put their fastest two swimmers on first. The speedy Roland Schoeman gave them a substantial lead on the first leg, and the South Africans built on this lead through to the third leg. They used their fast swimmers to get ahead of the competition and benefit from less turbulent water. The USA finished third.

Team Spirit

In 2008, it was the USA's turn. Swimming in the next lane to the much-fancied French team, the USA showed great team spirit when Jason Lezak went into the final takeover 0.59 seconds down on Alain Bernard (France), who just a few days later was to become the individual 100m Freestyle champion. Lezak's takeover was good but he made little impact at first. Going into the final turn, he was beginning to gain on Bernard and, as Bernard started to slow down, he quickly reeled him in, overtaking him over the last two metres. This event underlined the fact that people can become different swimmers in relays. When presented with team pressures, some get better, some perform worse.

Training for Competition

Regular practice and team interaction can help to develop team spirit and the takeover-sharpness needed. The fact that the swimmer taking over can be in motion as the incoming swimmer completes his or her swim means that, except for the lead swimmer, a relay swim can be half a second to a second faster than the same distance and stroke made in an individual event. The main aim should be to practise starts until, without becoming disqualified, you can consistently anticipate and start to move as early as possible. The best way to achieve this is by devoting training time to the relay.

If you are left in a position where you need to close a gap in a relay race, try not to chase too fast over the first part of your leg. Leave 'something in the tank' for closing that gap as your opponent tires.

Relay swimmers respond to team pressures in different ways.

The big day

For many people, the first swimming competition can be both an eagerly anticipated and a nerve-wracking experience. The advent of Masters swimming has meant that many people in adulthood are starting to race for the first time. Whatever age you are, the excitement of the first competition remains the same.

Race day

Entering a competition requires planning and preparation. At international level, swimmers not only taper their training but shave off their bodyhair to maximise their sharpness. That may be a step too far at lower levels but some thought on rest, diet and other preparations are advisable.

Good planning is essential to success in racing. The first step is to be aware of how to enter competitions. In order to race, you will normally be required to be a member of an ASA club. If the club is accredited under the ASA's Swim21 scheme, you can be sure it is well-organised.

On the Day

National events generally require that you enter online, but competitions at county or club level may allow you to enter by post. When you arrive on the day, there is normally a number of ways of registering. Some organisers will adopt a system of heats, which are seeded beforehand. If you withdraw from an event, your lane will be left empty. For national events, withdrawal is normally only permitted on the day prior to the event. If you fail to withdraw, it is worth bearing in mind that you might be subject to a fine. The second option, which is normally adopted in club competitions, is that you merely sign in when you arrive.

Occasionally, you may find that an entry-card system is used. This requires you to complete an entry card at the competition, which is usually located in an entry box in the pool foyer or entrance to the changing rooms. Posting your card in this box is a form of 'secondary entry',

a statement that you intend to swim. At an announced time, the box is closed and the card entrants seeded into heats. This third system is little used. Your club should be able to help guide you with any of these systems.

In Masters swimming competitions for people aged 18 years and over, you can enter competitions with a temporary ASA membership, or as 'unattached' if the local promoter accepts your entry. Masters competitions also generally use the pre-seeded process, although entries for 400 and 800 metres events can sometimes be made through a check-in desk.

Tapered Training

In the period leading up to your first race, your training should change in composition. Over the last two to three weeks, which is often called the taper period due to swimmers tapering off their training, you will need to rest as much as possible between training sessions. You will need to give your body more time to regenerate following the hard work you have been putting in during the previous months. Try to go to bed earlier and sleep for longer. Increase both the pace of each training swim and the amount of rest between each swim or repetition. At the same time, steadily decrease the number of repetitions and overall

training distance swum
per session.

If you normally
supplement your work
in the water with land
conditioning, decrease the
levels of strength training but
keep your flexibility training
going. Getting the balance
right between all these factors
is difficult and you are unlikely
to get it absolutely right on the
first occasion. Most swimmers
judge what type of taper
suits them best through trial
and error. A lot of swimmers,
for example, prefer to
taper off only a few days
before competition.

There are several factors that
will have a general effect on
your taper, such as the amount
of training you have completed
over the last year, and your
strength and age. Remember that
you are trying to arrive at a peak,
and mentally preparing for the
competition will help achieve this.
You will also need to undertake
sharpening work over very short
distances to practise your starts and
turns. Aim to arrive at the race day
in a state of being physically and
mentally more relaxed than at any
time during the year.

*Tapering your training in the run-up to
a competition will help to maximise
your performance.*

Race day

Confirming or registering your entry and familiarising yourself with the pool, starting blocks and turning walls are among the first issues to be dealt with when you arrive at the competition venue. It's also important to go in with a race plan based on your recent training and race targets.

Everyone has a different approach to the race day. Most swimmers have a range of rituals that they go through, but since this will be the first of hopefully many races, you will not have any experiences to fall back on. The following information is a series of tips that you can later adopt or discard according to whether you feel they have worked or not.

Acclimatising Your Body

Start by rising sufficiently early so that your body is acclimatised. Based on the time of the competition session, you will need to determine when you should get up. A short, very easy walk will help to get the body's metabolism working well. During this period, you need to set aside time to think through your race strategy for later in the day. Will you go out fast? Will you rely on consistent splits? Are you likely to be drawn against someone you know, and therefore able to pace yourself accordingly?

Eating and Drinking

Avoid eating within 2 hours of the start of your race. This may well limit you to just breakfast in the morning. During breakfast, opt to eat plenty of carbohydrates, such as porridge, muesli and low-fat yoghurts. These foods can be digested quickly and, being carbohydrate, will provide much of the energy you need for your muscles to work. It is always a good idea to avoid fatty foods on the day of a race. The reason for this is that, while fats contribute towards providing the energy needed, particularly in distance races, they take some time to digest and will contribute less on the day.

The importance of drinking water also needs to be recognised. Although you will be swimming in water, you can quickly become dehydrated, particularly if you are sitting and waiting to compete on the poolside.

Packing for the Race

Also, give yourself sufficient time to pack your bag for the meet or make sure that you pack the night before. It is a good idea to create a checklist. You will probably be distracted on the race day and a list may be a useful aid. Typically, among other things, you will need to remember warm poolside clothing, training shoes, two or three swimming costumes, a swim-cap, goggles and food.

Warming Up

Following your journey to the competition pool, you may well be stiff so a reasonable warm-up is needed. Your warm-up should open the blood vessels

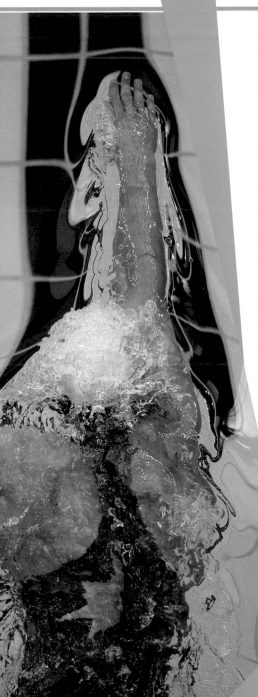

to the muscles to be used in the race, and lift your pulse rate. This warm-up should consist of some poolside stretching exercises and a good 20 minutes to half an hour in the water.

Try to perform your session in the water as close to the time of the actual swim as possible. The session should consist of easy swimming with at least two strokes, starts and turns practice, and some short sprinting, which should also include starts. You will need to familiarise yourself with the starting blocks and, if you are swimming backstroke, the position of the backstroke start handles and flags. You will also need to think about the pool wall, whether there is guttering at the wall and the height of the water in relation to the wall. Also, determine whether the walls are likely to make your feet slip on turning.

A breakdown of how you might distribute your warm-up time might be as follows:

- 5–10 minutes of stretching exercises, concentrating particularly on ankles and shoulders;
- 10 minutes of fartlek (swimming at variable speeds over a distance) or easy swimming;
- 5 minutes of short sprint work;
- 5 minutes of starts and turns;
- 5 minutes of loosening down.

Include some start and turn practice in your warm-up.

How swimming is organised

Swimming truly is a sport for life, perhaps more than any other. There are opportunities to compete at every age and at most levels of ability. But the way swimming is organised in the UK takes a bit of explaining.

Governing Bodies

Great Britain has a unique place in the global history of swimming, having spawned the sport's first governing body, the ASA, in 1869, and also hosted the inaugural meeting of FINA, the world governing body, in 1908. But the ASA only has jurisdiction over England. Scotland and Wales have their own governing bodies: Scottish Swimming (SASA) and Swim Wales (WASA). These three bodies run most of swimming's domestic affairs and are also responsible for the teams that compete as separate nations in the Commonwealth Games.

At the Olympic Games and European and world championships, however, the nations field a single team representing Great Britain, hence the need for an additional governing body. British Swimming is responsible for matters relating to Great Britain teams, although it shares some administrative staff with the ASA.

Ireland is unusual in that Northern Irish swimmers not only share a governing body, Swim Ireland, with fellow swimmers in Ireland, but compete with them internationally rather than as part of a Great Britain and Northern Ireland team. In the Commonwealth Games, however, Northern Ireland competes as a separate nation, without the Ireland swimmers, whose country is not part of the Commonwealth.

Domestic Competitions

In Britain, the annual calendar of domestic competitions includes age group, youth and senior championships at club, county, regional and national level, as well as a range of open meets hosted by clubs that are often targeted at specific levels of ability. Many of these competitions, including regional and national championships, publish qualifying times that swimmers must have achieved in order to enter.

Swimming tends to be an individual sport, but the team ethos comes to the fore in league competitions, most notably the National Arena Swimming League. Four

Many masters competitions now include an 18–24 years category.

hundred teams comprising a total of 16,000 swimmers compete in seven regional leagues across England and Wales. The seven champions, seven runners-up and next-best six teams go into national A and B finals each year.

For adults, Masters swimming has become very popular since its launch in the 1970s. Masters events are usually organised in five-year age bands from 25–29 upwards, though most

competitions now also feature an 18–24 category. The Masters calendar includes county, regional, national, European and world championships, and an ample supply of open meets. British Masters records are held for every age group up to 95–99. Internationally, there are even men's and women's world records for the 100–104 category.

Index

Acknowledgements

The authors gratefully acknowledge all those who have lent their knowledge and skills in the preparation of this book, in particular: Nick Sellwood, ASA head of England talent development; Chris Nesbit, GB head coach at the short-course World Championships 2008 and England head coach at the Commonwealth Games 2010; Mark Perry, British Swimming open water performance manager; Paul Hogg, head coach of the ASA Beacon programme at Portsmouth and Portsmouth Northsea Swimming Club; Dr Ian Gordon, ASA head of medical services and GB team doctor; Dr Ian Maynard, professor of sport psychology, Sheffield Hallam University; Nick Juba, head coach, Hatfield Swimming Club; Pat Dunleavy, former head physiotherapist, GB swim team; Diane Elliot, physiotherapy and sports science co-ordinator for ASA England talent development; Martin MacDonald of Mac-Nutrition.com, consultant nutritionist and adviser to the ASA; Bronwin Carter, athetics and weight-lifting coach and land training adviser to Portsmouth Northsea SC and the ASA Beacon programme at Portsmouth; Ian Mackenzie, secretary, National Arena Swimming League; Keely Downend, subscriptions manager and editorial assistant, *Swimming Times*.

Picture credits

The publishers would like to thank the following sources for their kind permission to reproduce the pictures in this book.

Action Images: /Brandon Malone: 41, 90-91; /Jason O'Brien: 74-75; /Reuters: 49, 50-51; /Aly Song/Reuters: 113

Getty Images: /Al Bello: 36-37, 98; /Bloomberg: 9; /Martin Bureau/AFP: 107, 118-119; /Tim Clary/AFP: 102, 105; /Chris Cole: 106; /Mark Dadswell: 34-35, 65; /Tony Duffy: 104; /Darren England: 114; /Laurent Fievet/AFP: 47, 111; /Jeff Gross: 60-61; /Alexander Hassenstein/Bongarts: 100; /Harry How: 123; /Hulton Archive: 14-15; /Michael Kappeler/AFP: 109, 115; /Keystone: 18; /Nick Laham: 58-59; /Streeter Lecka: 82-83; /Francois-Xavier Marit/AFP: 117; /Ryan Pierce: 20; /Popperfoto: 19; /Adam Pretty: 5, 7, 39, 56-57, 121, 125; /Rischgitz: 16; /Clive Rose: 66-67; /Marc Serota: 23; /Cameron Spencer: 33, 54, 108; /Nick Wilson: 101; /Greg Wood/AFP: 53

Press Association Images: /Sven Simon/DPA: 103